OSPREY AIRCRAFT OF THE ACES 115

ACES OF THE 78th FIGHTER GROUP

SERIES EDITOR: TONY HOLMES

OSPREY AIRCRAFT OF THE ACES 115

ACES OF THE 78th FIGHTER GROUP

Thomas McKelvey Cleaver

OSPREY
PUBLISHING

Front Cover
Maj Gene Roberts, CO of the 78th Fighter Group's 84th Fighter Squadron, shoots down the second of three German fighters on his way to becoming the first US pilot to claim a trio of victories in one combat on 30 July 1943. This is the most important date in the history of VIII Fighter Command, as for the first time American fighters found and attacked superior enemy fighter forces over Germany, scoring heavily with minimal losses and protecting the bombers. Due to a tailwind, the P-47 pilots of the 78th FG had met the Luftwaffe over Haltern, 50 miles further east into Germany than Eighth Air Force fighters had previously managed. Mission leader Maj Gene Roberts recalled;

'We were outnumbered by at least three-to-one, but were able to manoeuvre into attacking position with very little difficulty. The main reason for this success was that the German fighter pilots and Luftwaffe high command did not believe we could possibly be that far inland, and were not expecting to see a defensive force at all.'

After shooting down one Fw 190, Roberts spotted two more. 'They were about 2000 yards in front of me, heading out so that they could peel off and come back through the bomber formation'. Using the same tactic as before, Roberts closed so fast that he had to pull up and roll in on the second fighter in order to avoid a collision. 'I opened fire from dead astern. I observed several strikes and, as before, the enemy fighter billowed smoke and flames, rolled over and spun down'. After an intense ten minutes, the Thunderbolt pilots broke off combat while they still had fuel to return to their Duxford home. Their German opponents had failed to bring down any more bombers once they were engaged by the 78th FG. At a cost of seven P-47s lost in the melee, the group was credited with 16 victories (*Cover artwork by Mark Postlethwaite*)

First published in Great Britain in 2013 by Osprey Publishing
Midland House, West Way, Botley, Oxford, OX2 0PH
43-01 21st Street, Suite 220B, Long Island City, NY, 11101, USA

E-mail: info@ospreypublishing.com
Osprey Publishing is part of the Osprey Group
© 2013 Osprey Publishing Limited

A CIP catalogue record for this book is available from the British Library

ISBN: 978 1 78096 715 8
PDF e-book ISBN: 978 1 78096 717 2
ePub ISBN: 978 1 78096 716 5

Edited by Tony Holmes
Cover Artwork by Mark Postlethwaite
Aircraft Profiles by Chris Davey
Index by Alan Thatcher
Originated by PDQ Digital Media Solutions, UK
Printed in China through Asia Pacific Offset Limited

13 14 15 16 17   10 9 8 7 6 5 4 3 2 1

Osprey Publishing is supporting the Woodland Trust, the UK's leading woodland conservation charity, by funding the dedication of trees.

www.ospreypublishing.com

ACKNOWLEDGEMENTS
I would like to acknowledge the assistance and support of Col Richard E Hewitt (USAF Ret'd), Lt Col Huie H Lamb (USAF Ret'd), Dr Ernie Russell PhD and Capt Wayne E Coleman, pilots of the 78th FG, for their generous efforts in providing documentary material, photographs and, most importantly, their memories, as well as the time they took to read the manuscript and ensure its accuracy. Thank you also to Rusty Brown, nephew of Maj Quince Brown, for material and photographs provided regarding his late uncle. And, finally, Curt Shepherd, webmaster of the 78th FG website, for his unstinting efforts to provide photographs and personal contacts. This book would not exist otherwise. The editor would like to thank John M Dibbs, Robert F Dorr, Frank Olynyk and Peter Randall (www.littlefriends.co.uk) for the provision of photographs.

CONTENTS

30 JULY 1943

O n 30 July 1943 'Little Blitz Week' came to its conclusion, thus marking the end of the first sustained air offensive by the Eighth Air Force against Germany proper since the USAAF had commenced operations from southern England nearly a year earlier. This was the opening blow of the Combined Bomber Offensive that would see B-17 Flying Fortresses and B-24 Liberators finding targets over the next ten months in preparation for the Allied cross-Channel invasion and the eventual liberation of Europe.

Good flying weather in the latter part of July had allowed 14 strikes to be flown over the six days from 24 July. On the 30th, the Eighth Air Force's heavy bombers had targeted the Focke-Wulf factory at Kassel, having previously attacked similar plants in Oschersleben and Warnemünde during 'Little Blitz Week'. All three missions had seen the 'heavies' undertake deep penetration strikes beyond the range of escort fighters, and they drew maximum opposition from the defending Luftwaffe.

The 186 B-17Fs sent to attack Kassel on 30 July were already headed into the prevailing westerly wind at 22,000 ft as they released their bombs over the target and came out of the flak umbrella over the city, headed for home. In a matter of minutes, more than 100 Bf 109s and Fw 190s from JGs 1 and 11 made their presence known, as the contrails streaming from the American formation were easy for the German pilots to spot. Several formations slashed through the bomber boxes in 'Twelve o'clock high' attacks. Gunners aboard the Flying Fortresses fired at the grey fighters streaking past them, their cannon flashing. Bombers were hit, with three bursting into flames and falling out of formation. The sky was filled with blossoming parachutes. A B-17 in the lead box took hits in an engine and eventually fell behind after its crew had tried, forlornly, to keep up with the formation for protection.

P-47C-2 41-6243 was amongst the first batch of Thunderbolts assigned to the 84th FS in the spring of 1943. Christened *"Pappy"* **sometime after this photograph was taken from a 91st BG B-17F on 11 June 1943, the fighter was assigned to Capt George Hays (***USAAF***)**

Maj Jesse Davis, deputy CO of the 83rd FS, his crew chief MSgt Albert Ron (left) and assistant crew chief Roderick Wallace pose with their P-47C-2 41-6402 *Owley and Tobe*. The fighter proudly displays a victory symbol denoting the Fw 190 that Davis destroyed on 1 July 1943. He would claim his second, and last, kill in 41-6402 on 27 September. Note the early 200-gallon non-droppable ferry tanks fitted to the aircraft in the background. P-47C-5 41-6373 'HL-Z' was the mount of 83rd FS CO Lt Col James Stone, who claimed victories with it on 14 May and 30 July 1943 (*USAAF*)

At 23,000 ft over the English Channel, 15 miles west of the Dutch coast, 48 pilots of white-nosed P-47C/D Thunderbolts of the 78th Fighter Group (FG) climbed to cross into enemy air space at 29,000 ft. As future nine-kill ace Maj Gene Roberts, subsequently recalled;

'We started with the usual 48 fighters – three squadrons with 16 fighters each. However, two of the pilots reported mechanical problems and had to abort as we crossed the English Channel. In each case, per our standard procedure at that time, I had to despatch the aborting aeroplane's entire flight of four to provide an escort back to base. That left us with 40 fighters for the mission by the time we reached Holland.'

The 40 Thunderbolts came in north of Rotterdam, flying over Nijmegen before entering German airspace for the first time ever over Kleve. From this altitude, pilots could see the city of Haltern on the horizon. This was the deepest penetration of Germany yet made by American fighters, and it had been facilitated by a lucky tailwind at altitude. Only the day before the P-47-equipped 4th FG, using the troublesome, unpressurised belly tanks for the first time, had also made it as far east as the German border.

The task for the 78th FG pilots on 30 July was withdrawal support for the 'heavies' as they left Germany, after which the 'Debden Eagles' of the 4th FG would cover the B-17s' final withdrawal across the Channel to England.

Brand-new 78th FG commander Lt Col Melvin F McNickle flew beside Maj Roberts, CO of the 84th Fighter Squadron (FS), as 'White Three' element lead on this, his first mission. Deputy group commander Lt Col James Stone was 'Red One' of the second flight, while future five-kill ace Capt Jack C Price, who had claimed his first victory (an Fw 190) on 14 July, was 'Blue One' of the third. Fellow future 14.333-victory ace 1Lt Quince L Brown, victor in his first aerial combat a month previous, was 'Yellow One', leading the fourth flight. His wingman, Flt Off Peter Pompetti, also had a victory to his name – the first of an eventual seven kills.

Above Roberts' 84th FS was the 83rd FS as high cover, with future five-victory ace Capt Charles P London leading the unit as 'Red One'. He was the group's top scorer at that time with three kills. Finally, the 82nd FS, led by Maj Harry Dayhuff (another single-victory pilot), was in the low position.

Near Haltern, rocket-armed Bf 110G twin-engined fighter destroyers attacked the Flying Fortresses from the rear, firing missiles outside the range of the bombers' defensive fire and downing a B-17. At that moment the 78th FG saw the bombers approaching Haltern, just as Roberts spotted the German fighters;

'We were outnumbered by at least three-to-one, but were able to manoeuvre into attacking position with very little difficulty. The main reason for this success was that the German fighter pilots and Luftwaffe high command did not believe we could possibly be that far inland, and were not expecting to see a defensive force at all.'

Maj Eugene Roberts, CO of the 84th FS, gestures to the press from the cockpit of his P-47C-5 41-6630, *Spokane Chief* during a photo-call at Duxford following his triple victory haul of 30 July 1943. He was the first VIII Fighter Command pilot to down three aircraft in a single mission. This fighter, like all P-47Cs delivered to the 84th FS in the spring of 1943, was polished with beeswax to improve its airspeed as directed by Maj Roberts. Groundcrewman Sgt James Tudor recalled, 'It was easy to forget about the wax and slip, fall off the wing with a full tool box or take off the heavy bottom cowl section and have it slip through your fingers and come crashing down on your foot. I believe that the waxing gave the aeroplanes a whole 2-5 mph increase in speed!' (*USAAF*)

The Thunderbolt pilots quickly engaged the enemy fighters as they continued to target the bombers heading west, as Roberts subsequently recalled;

'There was one B-17 beneath the main formation, and it was being attacked by around five German fighters. The bomber was pouring smoke and appeared to be in deep trouble. From my position in the lead of the group, I dove down on the enemy fighters that were attacking the cripple. However, the Germans saw us, broke away, and dove for the ground. There wasn't much more we could do to help the crippled B-17, so I pulled up on the starboard side of the main bomber formation, about 1000 yards out. I discovered on reaching this position that my second element – Lt Col McNickle and his wingman – had broken away and was no longer with me. I had only myself and my wingman, Flt Off Glenn Koontz. We immediately saw enemy aircraft ahead of us and above the formation. I judged that there were more than 100 enemy aircraft in the area, as compared with our 40.'

Unknown to Roberts, McNickle had suffered an oxygen failure in P-47D 42-7961/WZ-M and collided with his wingman 1Lt James Byers. Upon their return to base, other members of the group reported seeing a P-47 in a steep dive. Incredibly, McNickle survived the resulting crash, regaining consciousness to find his aeroplane inverted, with members of the Dutch Resistance attempting to free him. With two broken shoulders and other serious wounds, he was turned over to the Germans, who denied him medical care for several days in an attempt to get information. Eventually, McNickle emerged from captivity in 1945. Byers perished in the collision, however.

Roberts and Koontz came across a gaggle of Fw 190s;

'Dead ahead of me was a single Fw 190, at the same level as Koontz and me, about 1000 to 1500 yards ahead. He was racing in the same direction as the bombers so he could get ahead of them, swing around in front and make a head-on pass. The bombers were most vulnerable from dead ahead. The Germans referred to this tactic as "queuing up".'

Roberts dove slightly below the enemy fighter to avoid being spotted, then closed to around 400 yards, where he opened fire, hitting the German heavily with a three- to five-second burst. 'The Focke-Wulf's wheels dropped and it spun down in smoke and flames'. Roberts then

Capt Charles London of the 83rd FS was credited with two victories on 30 July flying his P-47C-2 41-6335 *El Jeepo*. These successes took his final tally to exactly five kills, thus making him the first ace of VIII Fighter Command. Standing behind London in this photograph is his crew chief, TSgt Percy Scott (*USAAF*)

spotted two more. 'They were about 2000 yards in front of me, heading out so they could peel off and come back through the bomber formation'. Using the same tactic as before, Roberts closed so fast he had to pull up and roll in on the second fighter to avoid colliding with it. 'I opened fire from dead astern. I observed several strikes and, as before, the enemy fighter billowed smoke and flames, rolled over and spun down'. Amazingly, Roberts and Koontz were still in the middle of the action;

'After the second engagement we were about two miles ahead of the bombers and some 500 ft above them, still well out to their starboard side. Koontz was on my right wing. About this time, I observed a '109 on the port side and ahead of the bomber formation. I dropped below the bomber formation, crossed over to the port side and pulled up behind him, again at full throttle.'

As Roberts closed on his third enemy fighter, the Bf 109 suddenly executed a starboard 180-degree turn to attack the bombers head on;

'I closed to within 400 or 500 yards and opened fire. He was in a tight turn, and that required deflection shooting. My first two bursts fell away behind him, but I continued to close. I fired my third burst as he straightened out to approach the bombers.'

This caught the Messerschmitt from dead astern within 150 yards of the bombers. The fighter fell over into a spin, trailing smoke and flame. As Roberts despatched his third victim of the mission, wingman Glenn Koontz flamed the wingman his flight lead had failed to spot.

'We were now at the same level as the bombers, and approaching them from head-on', Roberts explained. 'We had no alternative but to fly between the two main formations, which were about two miles apart. Bless their hearts, they did not fire'. He then spotted two Bf 109s attacking a P-47;

'They were all heading 180 degrees to me, so I couldn't close effectively to help. I did fire a burst at the leading German, but without enough deflection. The P-47 dove and took evasive action. I didn't see him or the Germans again. I headed out and joined up with a loose element from the 84th, and we headed home together.'

Gene Roberts had just scored the first triple victory haul by an Eighth Air Force fighter pilot.

The rest of the 78th FG had been just as busy as Roberts. Top-scorer Charles London caught two Fw 190s at 26,000 ft, flaming one and diving to avoid the wingman. Zooming back to 28,000 ft, he hit the engine of a Bf 109, setting it on fire. With this, Capt Charles London became the first ace of the Eighth Air Force.

Quince Brown and Peter Pompetti hit a flight of four Bf 109s, with Brown damaging the lead fighter and Pompetti firing on the remaining three. He then executed a high-G turn, which left five of his guns jammed. Despite having only three still working, Pompetti hit the cockpit of the right wingman and killed the pilot. He then had to break off his attack to avoid a collision.

Capt Jack Price found a flight of Fw 190s and flamed the leader. Turning into the enemy element leader, Price and his wingman, 2Lt John Bertrand, each hit two of the three remaining Focke-Wulfs, both of which went down out of control. 82nd FS CO Maj Dayhuff spotted a Bf 109 making a beam attack on the bombers, so he closed astern the German machine and blew it up with a concentrated burst of fire. Deputy group commander Lt Col Stone also hit a Bf 109, which blew up so close to his P-47 that both he and his wingman, 2Lt Julius Maxwell, flew through the explosion.

After an intense ten minutes, the Thunderbolt pilots broke off combat while they still had fuel to return to their Duxford home. Their German opponents had failed to bring down any more bombers once they were engaged by the 78th FG. At a cost of seven P-47s lost in the melee, the group was credited with 16 victories. Coupled with the eight credited to the 56th and 4th FGs, the day's battles had doubled VIII Fighter Command's total score in the war to date.

30 July 1943 is the most important date in the history of VIII Fighter Command, as for the first time American fighters found and attacked superior enemy fighter forces over Germany, scoring heavily with minimal losses and protecting the bombers.

30 July 1943 also witnessed another harbinger of the future. Chased to the deck by two Fw 190s that he finally outdistanced, 1Lt Quince Brown headed for the Channel coast, following railway lines. Near Leiden, in Holland, he spotted a train and strafed it, leaving the engine wreathed in steam. It was the first strafing attack by an American fighter, and a preview of what would eventually become the main activity of American fighter pilots during the final year of the war, particularly for Quince Brown and the 78th FG.

For the Luftwaffe, the writing was on the wall.

P-47C-2 41-6335 was photographed visiting an unidentified bomber airfield just prior to the historic 30 July mission. Although there are four victory symbols beneath the fighter's cockpit, only three of these were for confirmed kills. The first denoted an Fw 190 probable London claimed on 14 May. When VIII Fighter Command's first ace completed his tour in November 1943, 41-6335 was passed on to replacement pilot Lt John Johnson. He used it to claim an Fw 190 destroyed and a second fighter damaged over Dusseldorf on 22 February 1944, only to be shot down by another Focke-Wulf on his way home when the group was bounced near Eindhoven, in Holland. Johnson bailed out and became a PoW (*USAAF*)

BEGINNINGS

I t had been an article of faith that the US Army Air Corps (USAAC) believed the doctrine of Douhet and Trenchard – 'the bomber will always get through' – throughout the interwar years. This manifested itself in the belief that the Eighth Air Force would be able to operate over Germany with 'self-defending' bombers once it committed aircraft to the European Theatre of Operations (ETO) from mid-1942. However, ever increasing losses proved the folly of this doctrine during the summer of 1943.

Indeed, the first signs that the USAAC's senior leadership was questioning the theories of Douhet and Trenchard came in the wake of the massacre of unescorted Wellingtons in December 1939, which resulted in RAF Bomber Command subsequently abandoning daylight bombing. Reports of this incident were closely studied by USAAC strategists, who also took a keen interest in the mauling of unescorted Luftwaffe bombers during the Battle of Britain in the summer of 1940. As a result of their findings, fighters were an integral part of the Eighth Air Force from the very beginning.

Only one US fighter was competitive with its German counterparts when America entered the war following the Japanese attack on Pearl Harbor in December 1941 – the Lockheed P-38 Lightning. Originally a high-altitude point defence interceptor, a P-38D equipped with two 160-gallon drop tanks had demonstrated potential as a long-range fighter. The 1st Pursuit Group (PG) had only received the first 13 pre-production YP-38s six months earlier. Thirty-six P-38Ds delivered in September had self-sealing fuel tanks and armour plate, and an additional 210 P-38Es remained in the delivery cycle. The fully mission-capable P-38F was still some way off in the future, however.

The Lightning was plagued by gremlins during the early phase of its service introduction. Possibly the most alarming of these faults was the fighter's unfortunate tendency to tuck its nose under in a dive, while controls stiffened as the angle-of-attack increased until the pilot was unable to pull out. Fowler manoeuvre flaps could also deploy differentially, causing the aeroplane to go inverted without notice.

On Friday, 5 December 1941, there were 69 P-38s of all sub-types on the USAAC roster. Two days later, in the wake of the Pearl Harbor attack, the USAAC created units to take the P-38 to the UK as rapidly as possible. The 1st PG lost more than half of its trained pilots and groundcrew between mid-December 1941 and early January 1942 to help man the newly created 14th and 82nd PGs.

On 7 January newly graduated pilot and future 78th FG stalwart 2Lt Robert Eby was transferred to the 49th Pursuit Squadron (PS) of the 14th PG. His squadron CO was 1Lt Arman Peterson, who was destined to become the 78th FG's first commanding officer. Eby recalled;

'That day, we transferred to Long Beach Airport to check out in P-38s. Of the other two squadrons in the group, one flew a mix of P-38s and elderly P-43 Lancers [precursor to the P-47] and the other was equipped with Vultee P-66 Vanguard fighters, which were terrible.'

The 14th PG, with 14 P-38s and an assortment of P-43 and P-66 fighters, was transferred to Hamilton Field, north of San Francisco, on 20 January 1942. 'We trained new pilots and prepared for overseas duty', Eby explained. 'Twice a week the call came down from Fighter Command to ship a certain number of pilots overseas the next day, which was done by drawing names out of a hat. We were one of two groups defending the northern West Coast, with the other at Paine Field, Washington. In the meantime, we were averaging more than one crash a week in the P-38, with most of those being fatalities. Pilot morale was low'.

On 9 February the 78th PG, consisting of the 82nd, 83rd and 84th PSs, was officially formed at Hamilton Field with an initial complement of half the pilots of the 14th PG. The 82nd had 24 enlisted men and seven pilots, and was commanded by 1Lt George Nash. By 27 March the number of enlisted men had risen to 92, but pilot numbers had dropped by one. 1Lt Frank Wagner was the group CO.

Lt Col Harry Dayhuff, who led the 82nd FS into combat in the ETO, was one of the original pilots assigned to the 78th FG in the weeks following the Pearl Harbor attack and the US entry into World War 2. He subsequently became a staff officer with the group after leaving the 82nd FS in mid-August 1943 (*USAAF*)

The 14th and 78th PGs continued to operate as one while their pilot ranks were fleshed out with new flight school graduates, most of whom had no twin-engined fighter experience. As newly promoted Capt Gene Roberts remembered, 'A high-time P-38 pilot in this period was one who could record his total time in the aircraft in low double digits!'

On 7 May Capt Armand Peterson, commander of the 49th Fighter Squadron (the term Pursuit was replaced by Fighter on 1 May 1942), was promoted to major and made CO of the 78th FG. 1Lt Harry Dayhuff arrived from Naval Air Station North Island, in San Diego, with three P-38s on 15 May, having lost 2Lt Wendell Seppich off La Jolla when he entered a cloud bank and crashed. Dayhuff became commander of the 82nd FS.

By 23 June the squadrons were operating from Hamilton Field, Oakland Airport and South San Francisco Airport. 'Our training was hit or miss until Maj Peterson organised the group, unified our goals and set it all down in writing', explained Dayhuff. Robert Eby, who became a staff officer with the 78th FG at this time, remembered;

'During this period all squadrons were constantly on alert, with one flight of four pilots in readiness with their aeroplanes warmed up and ready to scramble on receipt of orders from Fighter Command. One night I was out on a flight and we were notified that a Japanese submarine had been spotted off the Golden Gate Bridge. We managed to get there and identify the submarine as a fishing boat that was heading back to harbour.'

In June, Group Operations Officer 1Lt Morris Lee visited the 83rd FS at South San Francisco Airport. As he walked through the main hangar, he watched in horror as a P-38 crashed into a nearby maintenance building;

'Yelling for everyone to evacuate the hangar, I ran around to where the P-38 had crashed into the doorframe of the building. The pilot was a new trainee who had been shooting landings. He raised his body up from the cockpit and cried "Help me!" Before anyone could do anything, however, he was engulfed in flames. The fire caused the ammo in the fighter to start cooking off. Then boxes of 0.50- and 0.30-cal ammunition stored nearby started going off too. Several aeroplanes under repair in the hangar were soon aflame. Fire units from nearby communities took several hours to contain the major conflagration. I can still hear the pilot's helpless cry as he slumped back into the seat behind a wall of flames.'

This was one of many fatalities. 'At this time, we were losing approximately a pilot a month to fatal crashes', Lee explained. 'One I had to investigate north of Hamilton Field had hit the ground in a vertical dive. The two engines required a backhoe to retrieve them, as they had buried themselves ten feet into the ground. A jellied mass the size of two basketballs was all that was identifiable of the pilot'.

On 25 June the four fighter groups on the West Coast commenced their movement to England. The 1st FG began sending aircraft to England on 27 June, with six to eight P-38s being escorted by B-17s that provided navigation. The aircraft routed via Presque Isle (Maine), Goose Bay (Labrador), Bluie West One (southern Greenland) and Reykjavík (Iceland), with their final destination being RAF Goxhill, in Lincolnshire. On 15 July six P-38Fs from the 94th FS and their two B-17 escorts were forced down on a Greenland glacier. While all personnel were recovered safely, the aircraft were left behind and the plan to send fighters by air was immediately abandoned. The 1st FG moved to England by ship in late July, followed by the 14th FG in August.

As groups arrived in England, a momentous decision was made that would adversely affect the Eighth Air Force for the next year. Following President Franklin D Roosevelt's agreement with Prime Minister Winston Churchill for an Allied invasion of North Africa, units that had been sent to the Eighth Air Force in the UK were diverted to the Twelfth Air Force. On 23 September, the 1st FG, which was close to flying its first operational mission, was transferred – the 14th FG followed a week later. The 82nd FG arrived in England in November and was also reassigned to the Twelfth Air Force. The Eighth Air Force had lost its long range fighter escort groups just as they were ready to fly missions beyond the range of Spitfire support.

On 1 November the 78th FG set out for England, departing Oakland on 10 November bound for Camp Kilmer, in New Jersey. Amongst the personnel to arrive on the East Coast on 15 November was Robert Eby;

'Maj Peterson believed in advance planning. Before we left, we salvaged two large crates that had housed film-developing machines. The pilots and crews all chipped in and bought enough American booze to fill the crates, which were cleverly marked and shipped off with the other equipment. There must have been some breakage en route as only one crate was eventually delivered to Goxhill. We voted not to open it until Christmas.'

On 23 November the group boarded the liner *Queen Elizabeth* with 12,000 other American soldiers, sailors, fliers (French, British and American) and 300 nurses. The 78th duly arrived in Scotland just six days later, disembarking for Goxhill on 30 November.

Unofficially nicknamed 'Goat Hill', Eighth Air Force Station No F-345 Goxhill field had been built by the RAF in 1941. All new USAAF units sent to the UK received ETO indoctrination here from August 1942. In a letter home, NCO Earl Payne recalled Nissen hut living as '16 beds and one teeny-weeny coal stove, no latrines or water within a mile, and 25-watt bulbs for "illumination". The sun hardly ever shines, the days are short and lately it's very cold and windy'.

P-38Gs began to slowly arrive at Goxhill from mid-December, but in late January 1943 word reached the unit that all of its Lightnings were to be immediately sent to North Africa as attrition replacements. With his group temporarily lacking aircraft, Maj Peterson, who by now had been named station commander at Goxhill and promoted to lieutenant colonel, arranged to send pilots to RAF airfields for 'familiarisation'.

83rd FS flight commander Capt Charles London led a handful of pilots to Hornchurch, in Essex. Once at the RAF fighter airfield, its Wing Commander Flying, Wg Cdr A M Bentley, 'wondered what we were supposed to do', London recalled. 'We said he was supposed to teach us to fight the war, so he got us checked out in Spitfire Mk IXs. I got about 45 minutes in one, and then he said "Tomorrow we'll go on a Do"!' The next morning the Americans flew to Calais. Later that day 'we were about to take off on another mission to see if we could goad the Hun into a reaction when a teletype came in stating we were not supposed to fly. This was very embarrassing, as Bentley was only supposed to tell us war stories!'

Prior to the departure of the Lightnings, Harry Dayhuff took one up for a test flight and decided to buzz the field. Making a successful run he then went in again, only lower. Two more runs had his propellors nearly clipping the grass as he got closer and closer to the operations shack. When he landed, his armourer Warren Kellerstadt praised his flying, and commented that he had done a good job of missing the telephone pole right next to the shack. Dayhuff went white when he saw the 20-ft pole, which he had not seen at all while buzzing the field.

On 15 January, Peterson had informed the group's pilots that they would begin performing escort missions against the U-boat pens at Lorient and Brest, in France. Just days later, as previously noted, word reached Goxhill that high attrition amongst the P-38 groups in North Africa meant that the 78th's fighters would soon be taken away from them. The exodus of aircraft began before the end of January, with P-38s being sent a few at a time to the Lockheed Lightning Modification Depot at Langford Lodge, in Northern Ireland, for fitting with sand filters, prior to being ferried to North Africa. Pilots at Goxhill assumed that replacement P-38s would arrive shortly thereafter so as to avoid a lengthy delay in the group commencing operations. However, when four P-47C Thunderbolts flew in on 29 January it was obvious that the group would not be receiving any more Lightnings.

Few pilots in the 78th FG had ever seen a P-47, let along flown one. Curiosity, and suspicion, surrounding the Republic fighter mounted when two ferry pilots flying aircraft to Goxhill perished in separate crashes on 30 January. Charles London's first thought upon seeing a Thunderbolt at Goxhill was 'Thank God we don't have to fly those things!' being a confirmed P-38 flier. He soon learned otherwise. Ultimately, 'we didn't have any trouble transitioning to single engines because we had all previously flown P-40s. The P-47 was so much better than the P-40 that we didn't have a problem learning it at all', London explained.

Reading the manual for the Thunderbolt, pilots were struck by the dire warnings not to dive vertically from above 20,000-25,000 ft. On 6 February Capt Herb Ross (who would subsequently claim seven victories flying P-38s with the 14th FG in North Africa) of the 82nd FS took one up for a check ride. Climbing to 35,000 ft, he pushed over to see what all the fuss was about. Speed built up rapidly, and at 27,000 ft Ross experienced tail buffeting that was so intense the control column flailed out of his hands. Grabbing it as he sped through 20,000 ft, he later commented that the controls felt as if they were 'set in concrete'. Running out of options to arrest the dive, Ross began feeding in nose-up elevator trim as a last resort. As the fighter passed through 10,000 ft, with its pilot certain that his time had come, the racket stopped, the nose gradually came up and the Thunderbolt levelled off at 5000 ft.

Ross then called the Airfield Officer of the Day in the tower to ask whether he should land the badly damaged fighter or bail out. Told to bring it in so that the group could have a look at the P-47, the pilot was so shaken that he had to be helped from the cockpit on arrival. A short inspection certified the previously brand new aeroplane as 'Class 26' – damaged beyond repair. The paint had been stripped off the leading edges of all flying surfaces, the wing spars and vertical and horizontal stabilisers had been pulled back, the sheet metal had failed at the wing roots and most of the fabric on the elevators was hanging in tatters. As Harry Dayhuff recalled, 'It was the sickest looking lately-new P-47 one can imagine, having only collided with air'. Ross gained the nickname 'Rocket' following this incident.

On 7 February Lt Col Peterson was ordered to VIII Fighter Command HQ at Bushey Hall, in Hertfordshire. Several hours later he returned to Goxhill and told all officers to assemble in the briefing room at 1500 hrs. When Peterson and his staff entered the room, everyone could see from the look on his face that the news was not good. Voice shaking, Peterson informed them that all pilots in the group except group headquarters, squadron commanders and flight commanders were to be immediately transferred to North Africa to replace heavy combat losses, and personnel should be ready to depart the next morning.

Just as the 78th FG was about to enter combat as the first long-range fighter escort group in the Eighth Air Force after a year's preparation and training, it had lost its first choice fighters and the men that were supposed to fly them. Now equipped with a new aeroplane no one at Goxhill had previously flown, and awaiting the arrival of replacement pilots from the USA, the group's command cadre had to start over from scratch. And this time it would not have a year to get ready.

As of 8 February 1943, VIII Fighter Command was a shadow of what it was supposed to be. Only three fighter groups remained – the 4th, 56th and 78th. All would fly the P-47.

The unit that was most familiar with the big Republic fighter was the 56th FG, which had been the first USAAF group to be equipped with the Thunderbolt the previous June. Newly arrived in England, it was still getting organised at this time. The former RAF 'Eagle' squadrons, now re-designated and grouped together within the 4th FG, had combat experience, but in Spitfires rather than the P-47s they too had now been issued with. It was estimated by VIII Fighter Command that it would take the newly equipped groups two months to gain familiarity with the Thunderbolt. Then there was the 78th, which had neither familiarity with the P-47 nor operational experience, facing the high hurdles of recreating a fighter group. Regardless, pressure was on from the highest levels to whip things into shape and commence operations.

The Eighth Air Force had little option but to issue the 78th with Thunderbolts, despite the group's unfamiliarity with the aircraft. This was primarily because it was the only other American fighter besides the P-38 that could operate at high altitude – the optimum height for the B-17s and B-24s tasked with taking the fight to Germany. Thanks to the fighter's rather complex turbo supercharger, the P-47 could replicate its sea level performance at 28,000 ft. However, even with a phenomenal 307 gallons of internal fuel (the Spitfire VB, by comparison, could carry just 85 gallons), the Thunderbolt could only fly slightly beyond the coast of Holland or northern France from bases in East Anglia.

Additionally, the P-47 was designed to intercept high altitude transatlantic bombers attacking the USA – it was no dogfighter. With horizontal manoeuvrability compromised, the Thunderbolt had the lowest rate-of-climb of any American fighter. Later versions would use different propellors to give a 'dive-and-zoom' capability second to none, but in early 1943 the P-47 was defined more by what it could not do than what it could.

Pilots were ordered to remain at high altitude whenever possible and not engage in air combat below 20,000 ft, thus giving the P-47 a performance edge over German fighters. The problem was air combat did not work that way. An aeroplane that could not fight at whatever altitude it found itself at was not much use.

Pilots' opinions were divided. Those from the 56th FG believed in the P-47, and maintained that belief throughout the war, resisting moves for the group to switch to the P-51D/K Mustang in 1945. Future ace Maj Don Blakeslee, 336th FS commander within the 4th FG and the first pilot to score a victory with the P-47 in the ETO on 15 April 1943, compared it to the Spitfires he had previously seen considerable combat in and found the Republic fighter wanting. After diving from 28,000 ft onto three Fw 190s at 20,000 ft, he caught one that tried to out-dive him and had the satisfaction of seeing it explode under the weight of his fire at an altitude of 500 ft. Congratulated for proving the Thunderbolt could out-dive the Fw 190, he replied 'By God it ought to dive – it certainly won't climb!'

For the 78th, the leadership of Col Peterson, known as 'Colonel Pete' to his men, was vital. Staff officer Robert Eby recalled his CO's efforts;

'"Colonel Pete" put me in charge of bore-sighting the guns. I went to VIII Fighter Command to obtain the ballistic data and it took me three days with the various bureaucracies to find what we needed. I had to go through VIII Fighter Command, RAF Fighter Command and the British Air Ministry. I drew up alternate combinations of bore-sighting patterns and got the data from which to choose the best ones. "Colonel Pete" was way ahead of the other fighter groups on this, and when they went to the Air Ministry, they were told the "Yanks" had been given the data once and that was enough. VIII Fighter Command had to come to us and get our data.

Standing fourth from the left, Col Arman Peterson (78th FG CO) and Maj Eugene Roberts (84th FS CO), second from right, brief American war correspondents at Duxford following a mission in June 1943 (*USAAF*)

'I was very pleased when "Colonel Pete" told me, upon returning from a meeting at VIII Fighter Command with Cols 'Hub' Zemke from the 56th FG and Chesley Peterson from the 4th FG, that they had accepted our bore-sighting patterns. Subsequently, all P-47 groups in the ETO used them.'

Peterson also fought to improve the gunsight fitted to the P-47, also entrusting this task to Eby;

'The American gunsight had a 60 mph ring that was inadequate for the speeds at which aerial combat was fought in World War 2. "Colonel Pete" loved the beautiful 100 mph gunsight of the Spitfire, and when he tried to get them fitted to the P-47 he was turned down.'

Eby was able to obtain a 90 mph ring on a reticle, and found a local company that could recreate it. Nevertheless, Peterson did not give up on fitting the Thunderbolts with Spitfire gunsights, and he managed to obtain them just weeks before his group went operational. Non-magnetic mounts had to be fashioned for the British gunsights, since they were positioned directly above the P-47's magnetic compass – the standard mounts threw the compass off by 20-30 degrees.

Peterson's unceasing efforts to properly equip and train the pilots in his group, despite time pressures, forged a strong bond between him and his men.

Forty-five new pilots arrived at Goxhill on 16 February, many of them being US citizens who had joined the RAF or RCAF prior to America entering the war. One such individual was Harding Zumwalt, who recalled;

'On 11 February 1943 I reported to Eighth Air Force Combat Replacement Center 7 at Atcham airfield, in Shropshire, where we continued proficiency in Spitfires until transferring to Goxhill and the 83rd FS. There, I saw my first P-47, and it was quite impressive. The "Jug" weighed twice as much as the Spitfire and appeared large enough to house a couple of waist gunners in the rear. When I first taxied a P-47 it was just like driving a Cadillac, the fighter squatting on its gear when you hit the brakes.'

The Eighth Air Force had sent a request to the RAF in January 1943 that it be allowed to base its fighter groups at established British fighter stations, since there was a shortage of bomber-sized airfields in East Anglia and a need to access the more elaborate communications facilities found at such sites when conducting fighter operations. At the end of January the 78th FG was duly ordered to move to the RAF station at Duxford, in Cambridgeshire, with a follow-on transfer to Halesworth, near the Suffolk coast, scheduled for July. The move began on 24 March and was completed by 7 April.

Every American ever stationed at Duxford remembers it for the station's central steam heating system. Anyone who spent more than a night in a Nissen hut was well aware of just how cold it could be in England, and how lucky they were that their base possessed steam heating. The overwhelming majority of Eighth Air Force units were billeted either in Nissen huts or tarpaper barracks at newly constructed airfields that lacked sufficient coal supplies to allow personnel to get even remotely warm during the long winter months.

Duxford's history stretched back to 1918, when many of the buildings on site were constructed for the RAF by German prisoners of war. During the interwar years it had been the RAF equivalent of Wright Field, being home to the RAF's research and development unit, the Aeroplane and Armament Experimental Establishment. During the Battle of Britain in the summer of 1940 it was the base of the famous 'Bader Wing'.

Station Number 357-F, VIII Fighter Command, as Duxford was officially known, had a 2000 ft x 1600 ft grass strip that allowed 50 aircraft to get airborne in just five minutes, taking off in groups eight abreast. In the winter, however, the grass was overlaid with Marston matting that could accommodate only two fighters at a time. Ace Huie Lamb remembered that in the snowy winter of 1945, 'You made very certain to stay ahead of the takeoff swing and stay straight on the runway, or you were going into a snow bank that was frequently as deep as I was tall.'

A major change was made in group markings with the arrival of the P-47s. Heretofore, the group had used the standard USAAF marking scheme that saw individual aircraft given a specific number-in-squadron identifier. Once in the ETO, however, units assigned the Eighth Air Force had adopted the RAF system of a two-letter group identification with a single-letter aircraft-in-squadron identifier on either side of the national insignia on the rear fuselage.

P-47C-2 41-6246 of the 83rd FS was photographed during a visit to the 381st BG's Ridgewell home, in Essex, in June 1943. Note the fighter's shallow lower fuselage profile, denoting that the aircraft had not yet been plumbed to carry external fuel tanks. This machine was assigned to Capt Dwight Wilkes, who served with the group from June 1941 through to May 1944. As with all other P-47 units in the ETO, the 78th quickly adorned its fighters with white identity markings to distinguish the Thunderbolt from the other radial-engined fighter in widespread use in-theatre, the Fw 190. The identity markings consisted of a white ring 24 inches in chord applied to the extreme nose, a white stripe 16 inches wide at the mid-point of the horizontal stabilisers on both the uppersurfaces and undersides and a band 12 inches wide around the vertical fin and rudder, with its upper edge 18 inches from the top of the rudder (USAAF)

An early photograph of 1Lt Quince Brown, who had joined the 84th FS in April 1943 as a highly experienced 25-year-old former flight instructor with more than 1326 flying hours in his log book. Indeed, this figure was bettered only by Col Peterson, who had been in the USAAF four months longer (*USAAF via John M Dibbs/ Plane Picture Company*)

To confuse German intelligence, the 78th adopted the identification codes previously assigned to the 31st FG, which had been transferred to Twelfth Air Force control and sent to North Africa. Thus, 82nd FS fighters used 'MX' codes, P-47s of the 83rd FS bore 'HL' codes and the 84th FS marked its machines with 'WZ' codes. Additionally, to distinguish the Thunderbolt from the enemy's radial-engined fighter, the Fw 190, all aircraft carried a 24-inch white band on the forward cowling, with 15-inch white bands across the horizontal stabilisers and a 12-inch white band horizontally across the vertical fin and rudder.

Five weeks after arriving at Duxford, the 78th FG was ready for its first mission. On 13 April the 83rd FS accompanied the 4th FG on an early afternoon sweep along the French coast, with the 82nd FS doing the same thing in the early evening. Both were high altitude fighter sweeps that saw aircraft flying over Dunkirk, Furnes, St Omer and Calais. Charles London remembered, 'The Germans ignored us completely, not even bothering to shoot flak at us'.

Major excitement came during the second mission when the group's executive officer, Lt Col Joe Dickman, failed to carefully maintain the mixture control as he operated the throttle during the flight – a common error that brought down a number of P-47s in the ETO in 1943. The aircraft duly suffered a blown cylinder head over Calais, which in turn forced Dickman to abandon the fighter two miles offshore. Catching his right arm and dislocating it on the risers during the bailout, he had trouble discarding his parachute and deploying his dinghy once in the water. Pulling out his hunting knife to free himself, he accidentally punctured the dinghy! Once in the dinghy, Dickman then kept himself busy pumping it up one-handed so as to stay afloat. An RAF Air-Sea Rescue launch eventually reached him, its crew having had to carefully pick their way through the minefield Dickman had landed in.

On 15 April, Gene Roberts and the 84th witnessed Maj Blakeslee's pursuit and destruction of an Fw 190, as previously noted. Two missions a day were flown on 17 and 21 April, and on 29 April 36 aircraft were sent aloft in the 78th FG's biggest show of force to date.

18 April had seen the second arrival of replacement pilots, with 18 aviators trained on the P-47 in the US joining the group. Among them was a flight instructor who had been fighting to get out of Training Command for a year. Future ace 1Lt Quince Brown betrayed his Oklahoma origins when he opened his mouth. Ernie Russell, who would later fly as wingman and element leader to Brown, remembered;

'He could joke and had a little smile, but he was not brash or loud. However, you knew that he meant what he said and, if tested, would tell you what he thought – never loudly, but as matter of fact. He was not

prone to jest, but he did have a good sense of humour. Above all he was not a braggart. It just wasn't in his makeup. He was known by all in the squadron as one of the best pilots, although he would never tell you that – like a cowboy, "the proof was in the pudding".

'Brown had excellent vision – better than mine, and I had 20/10 vision. His peripheral vision, which was essential to seeing movement in the sky, was unequalled. He was also blessed with good judgment. All that, combined with the fact that he was an excellent shot, made him a superb fighter pilot.'

Born on 7 December 1917, Brown was the fifth of five sons, hence his name. Joining the USAAC in 1940, aged 23, he was commissioned as a second lieutenant and received his wings at Kelly Field, Texas, on 25 April 1941. Much to his frustration, Brown was then made an instructor at Randolph Field, Texas, on the basis of his demonstrated flying ability. When he finally arrived at Duxford in the spring of 1943, Brown was one of the older aviators in the 78th FG. And with a logged total of 1326 flying hours, he was also one of the most experienced pilots in this wartime organisation. Indeed, this figure was bettered only by Col Peterson, who had been in the USAAF four months longer. With more P-47 time than most of those leading the 78th, Brown was given a quick promotion to element leader by Gene Roberts when he reported to the 84th FS.

The first 48-aeroplane mission on 4 May was to the Brest Peninsula, which required a stop at St Just (formerly Land's End airport), in Cornwall, to refuel, before making the otherwise-uneventful sweep. Further missions on 7 and 13 May failed to rouse the Luftwaffe, but this was not the case the following day. The mission of 14 May was to escort 40 B-17s sent to attack targets in Belgium. Departing Duxford at 1235 hrs, the 78th arrived over the Belgian town of Saint-Nicolas to find the bombers under attack by Fw 190s. Leaving the 84th FS as high cover, Col Peterson led the 82nd and

Photographed at Duxford soon after being declared operational, pilots from the 84th FS pose in front of Maj Gene Roberts' P-47C-5 41-6630 *Spokane Chief*. Roberts is sat on the grass third from the left, while to his left is the 78th FG's future ranking ace Quince Brown (14.333 kills). Directly behind Roberts is Peter Pompetti (seven kills), and to Pompetti's left is Jack Price (five kills) (*via Aeroplane*)

Maj (seen here in the cockpit of his P-47C as a Lt Col) James Stone, CO of the 83rd FS, scored the 78th FG's first victory when he downed an Fw 190 northeast of the Belgian town of Saint-Nicolas on 14 May. Following the loss of Col Arman Peterson and Lt Col Harold McNickle in July 1943, Stone was promoted to group commander – a role he fulfilled until 22 May 1944 (*USAAF*)

83rd FSs in a diving attack that chased the German fighters directly into the bomber gunners' defensive fire. Moments later 83rd FS CO Maj James J Stone scored the group's first victory when he flamed an Fw 190. He then found himself alone over enemy territory, so he wisely set course for England.

Shortly after Stone had downed his Fw 190, Capt Robert Adamina of the 82nd FS also destroyed a Focke-Wulf fighter. Flt Off Samuel R Martinek of the 83rd FS then fell victim to an Fw 190, being forced to bail out. Adamina was hit too, and he took to his parachute as well. It was later learned that both men had been taken prisoner.

Element leader Capt Elmer F McTaggart avenged Martinek when the Fw 190 that had shot his squadronmate down swerved in front of him, allowing McTaggart to fire a solid burst into the fighter. The enemy pilot then made the mistake of trying to flee by diving for the ground. Closing rapidly on his quarry, McTaggart's next bursts hit the wings and fuselage. At 12,000 ft his opponent entered a 45-degree dive, at which point McTaggart fired again and the Fw 190 burst into flames. Having followed it down to observe the crash, he turned away 'on the deck' to head home but was then bounced by another Fw 190 – having no wingman, the first McTaggart knew that he was being chased was when tracers raced past his cockpit!

Attempting to evade, McTaggart hit a tree and the propellor cut through a telephone line. The ruggedness of the Thunderbolt saved him when he then hit a second tree, the fighter staying intact long enough for McTaggart to pull up to 1500 ft and bail out. He successfully evaded capture, however, arriving back in the UK on 21 June. 'Mac' McTaggart had been gone for just five weeks – a USAAF record for escape, evasion and return prior to the D-Day invasion.

On 15 May, the 78th FG flew to the coastal field at Horsham St Faith, in Norfolk, to refuel before setting off on a 'Rodeo' (the codename given for a mission composed of fighters only) off Amsterdam that saw flak down 2Lt Jack M Sandmeier of the 82nd FS – he was killed. The next day the group ran into more than 100 Fw 190s over Flushing, in Belgium. While the 82nd FS maintained high top cover, Gene Roberts led the 84th FS in to attack 60 Fw 190s. Flt Off Charles Brown soon found himself behind three German fighters, blowing up the 'tail-end Charlie' and flaming a second, before six more hit him from above and behind.

In a desperate dogfight, Brown was wounded in the foot, leg and head when his Thunderbolt blew up under the combined fire of the German fighters. Thrown clear of the aircraft by the explosion, he deployed his parachute and landed near Walcheren Island, off the Dutch coast. Brown was soon rescued by a German destroyer.

By then his squadronmate Capt John D Irvin had claimed a third Focke-Wulf destroyed. A second 'Rodeo' to Abbeville-St Omer that afternoon proved to be uneventful.

Eleven more missions had been flown by 26 May, all of which were ignored by the Luftwaffe to the group's dismay. A high point was the visit

by English singer Vera Lynn, who entertained the Americans on 21 May. Five days later Duxford played host to royalty when, at 1015 hrs, a maroon limousine appeared and proceeded to Group Headquarters. Here, the men stood to attention to receive HRH George VI and Queen Elizabeth, as the monarchs paid their first visit to an Eighth Air Force base. Eighth Air Force Commander Maj Gen Ira Eaker and VIII Fighter Command leader Brig Gen Frank 'Monk' Hunter accompanied the Royals as they inspected the base. Maj Stone's P-47C 41-6373/HL-Z, the first aircraft in the group to be credited with scoring a victory, was inspected, with His Majesty climbing into the cockpit. As he did so, a formation of 72 B-17s passed overhead.

By then the 78th had perfected a very effective method for launching and assembling quickly, as Harding Zumwalt of the 83rd FS recalled;

'Our procedure for departure was to assemble 48 aircraft at the eastern end of the field. Two flights each – eight aircraft – would line up and take off across the field, followed at 15-second intervals by the remaining flights. Once off the ground, you held your heading for two minutes before executing a 180-degree turn by flights. The one difficult part was that the No 2 aircraft in the flight had to drop down below and to the left of the flight lead while performing the turn. In a minute-and-a-half, all 48 aircraft were forming up on the group leader.

'With the weather sometimes down to 500 ft, we had to assemble quickly before we went into the clouds, which were often so thick a

On 26 May 1943 HRH George VI and Queen Elizabeth paid their first visit to an Eighth Air Force base when they went to Duxford. Standing on the balcony of the airfield's now famous watch office, VIII Fighter Command's Gen 'Monk' Hunter (sixth from right, with the moustache) speaks with the King, wearing the uniform of an RAF air marshal, while Col Arman Peterson (third from right) converses with the Queen. Moments after this photograph was taken the royal couple viewed a massed takeoff by 36 aircraft from the 78th FG (*USAAF*)

wingman could barely see his leader, even when tucked in tight. Each flight leader maintained a constant rate of climb until we broke out on top, which sometimes didn't happen till we reached 25,000 ft, but we would be in a reasonable group formation when we popped out.'

Fourteen missions were flown during June, nine of which were uneventful. On 13 June, the 78th ran into 20 enemy aircraft near Lumbres, in northern France. The German pilots they encountered proved to be very good, as they left their American opponents without any victories, and with Lt O R Brown of the 82nd FS dead and Lt D M Marshall of the 84th FS as a PoW. Several other P-47s landed back at Duxford badly shot-up.

Nine days later, when the 78th arrived at the rendezvous point over Walcheren Island to provide returning bombers with withdrawal support, they spotted the Flying Fortresses under attack from Fw 190s. As the German fighters attempted to dive away from the P-47s, 83rd FS pilots Capt London and Flt Off H S Askelson, as well as Col Peterson, who was leading the unit on this occasion, each claimed an Fw 190 destroyed. Squadronmate Lt T W Shepard downed a Focke-Wulf the following day when the 78th was bounced between Lille and Ostend during a 'Rodeo'.

On 29 June the group refuelled at RAF Ford, in West Sussex, in order to penetrate deep enough to meet the bombers attacking Villacoublay airfield, eight miles southwest of Paris. The B-17s were under fire from heavy flak and being attacked by Bf 109s when the group arrived. Capt Charles London scored his second and third victories when he chased two Messerschmitts through the bomber formation and saw them explode within seconds of each other, thus becoming the group's top-scorer at that time.

A short while later Flt Off Peter Pompetti, No 4 in the last flight of 83rd FS machines, spotted an Fw 190 below him. Failing to get a response from his flight leader after calling him several times, he split-essed onto the tail of the German fighter and gave it a burst, but missed. Upon

Flt Off Pete Pompetti was among the first reinforcements to reach the 78th FG in February 1943. Seen here seated on his P-47C-5 41-6393 *"Axe the Axis"* shortly after claiming his first victory on 30 July 1943, Pompetti was one of the most aggressive pilots in the group. Indeed, his keenness to take the fight to the enemy whenever possible nearly got him transferred as a result of his violation of strict group discipline when he broke formation in order to engage German fighters. Pompetti was promoted from flight officer to second lieutenant following his second victory (on 17 August) and was shot down and captured on 17 March 1944 while strafing Beauvais airfield. By then his tally stood at five aerial and two strafing victories (*USAAF*)

returning to base Pompetti was called before the squadron commander by his flight leader. When the latter was asked by Pompetti if his calls had indeed been heard, the flight leader responded in the affirmative. However, he then stated that Pompetti had broken formation and left his squadronmates exposed. Pompetti refused to back down. 'Exposed to what? My God, we were at 30,000 ft!' He would go on to become an ace, but would never be viewed by the group leadership as a 'disciplined pilot'.

1 July 1943 proved to be the 78th FG's blackest day during its early war period. Col Arman Peterson led 32 aircraft of the 83rd and 84th FSs on a 'Rodeo' to the Dutch coast in his P-47D 42-7948/MX-P *Flagari*, callsign 'Kingpost Leader'. As the formation approached enemy territory at

23

Bob Hope (seated here in Capt Bob Eby's P-47C-2 41-6249 *Vee Gail*) and singer and entertainer Frances Langford brought their USO show to Duxford on 2 July 1943 – the day after the loss of group CO Col Arman Peterson in combat. The 78th had been greatly affected by Peterson's death, Hope later recalling that 'it was the toughest house I played to in the entire war' (*USAAF*)

29,000 ft, just south of the Hook of Holland bandits were spotted to the right of the P-47s some 5000 ft below.

Peterson, leading a flight from the 84th FS, dove on four Fw 190s while unit CO Maj Gene Roberts took on four more German fighters immediately behind him. The fight quickly turned into a 'dive-and-zoom' battle, and three Fw 190s were claimed as destroyed, two as probables and two damaged. Missing his target, Peterson zoomed straight up into the late afternoon sun, blinding his wingman in the process and losing him in the glare. At this decisive moment, with no one covering his tail, Peterson dove again on the enemy, and was in turn hit by an unseen foe. There was no call on the radio, and no one saw 'Kingpost Leader' plunge into the North Sea off the Dutch town of Ouddorp.

One moment Peterson was their beloved commander, the next he had vanished forever. No future CO of the 78th would ever be so loved and respected by his men as the 28-year-old Peterson, who had brought them together in difficult circumstances the year before, trained them and turned them into an effective fighter group, only to have to repeat the process all over again shortly after the 78th arrived in England. Every pilot believed Peterson knew him and liked him, and they all knew he would do anything for them to ensure their success.

Even the visit the next day by comedian Bob Hope and singer and Hollywood actress Frances Langford with their USO troupe failed to lift the men's spirits, with Hope later recalling 'they were the toughest house I played to in the entire war'. For the next week, P-47s took off from Duxford to return to the area off Ouddorp, searching in vain for 'Colonel Pete'. His callsign, 'Kingpost', was permanently retired shortly after he was posted Missing in Action. 83rd FS CO Maj Stone was subsequently promoted to the rank of lieutenant colonel and given temporary command of the 78th, flying as 'Graywall Leader'.

Before Stone could settle in, however, Lt Col Melvin F McNickle arrived to assume command, with Stone becoming his deputy group commander. McNickle had spent time at Duxford in the autumn of 1941 when he had been an observer/liaison officer assigned to RAF Fighter Command's No 601 Sqn, then struggling to become operational with the Airacobra I. His twin brother was group commander of the P-39-equipped 350th FG in North Africa.

On 14 July Maj Harry Dayhuff led the 78th to Hornoy, in northern France, where they rendezvoused with B-17s attacking Amiens/Glisy airfield. Spotting Fw 190s over Montreuil heading for the bombers, Dayhuff led an attack that turned into a major fight.

Bounced by two Fw 190s that shot out the right side of his cockpit and instrument panel and caused splinter wounds in both hands, ankles and his right knee, 2Lt August DeGenero of the 82nd FS thought he was going to die. Having shaken off his attackers, he then got 'damned mad' and dove into another swarm of Fw 190s, shooting down one from 100 yards, probably destroying a second and damaging a third, before ducking into low clouds and heading for the Channel. Three vengeful German pilots followed him virtually to the French coast, DeGenero having to fly without instruments and controlling the Thunderbolt with his forearms only.

On the way home he lost his right aileron, and had to fight the damaged rudder and elevators to remain in control of the fighter. A crash landing was out of the question since he had unstrapped himself when he thought he would have to bail out after being shot up. He eventually spotted a fishing boat off the East Sussex port of Newhaven, and started circling it. The canopy was jammed and he was forced to batter it open with his injured hands. Finally able to bail out, DeGenero came down near the *Little Old Lady*, whose crew saved his life by pulling him out quickly, since he was unable to undo his parachute harness and was suffering from blood loss. A few weeks later he was awarded the Distinguished Service Cross (DSC), then sent home to recover.

Aside from DeGenero's victory, future five-kill ace Capt Jack Price of the 84th FS also claimed his first success during the 14 July mission when he downed an Fw 190 near Abbeville. Sadly, DeGenero's squadronmate Lt D G Jackson did not enjoy the same luck as him that day, as he was killed when his P-47C was shot down in error by defensive fire from a B-17.

Between 24-30 July the USAAF staged 'Little Blitz Week' – the Eighth Air Force's first attempt to maintain a sustained series of attacks against the German aviation industry. Good weather allowed 14 missions to be flown during the offensive. At the same time, VIII Technical Command began distributing 200-gallon centreline ferry tanks to the three fighter groups. While these unpressurised tanks could not be used above 20,000 ft, they enabled the fighters to cross the Channel without eating into the P-47's internal fuel supply, thus increasing the groups' radius of action by a very useful 50-60 miles. The big problem with them was that they could not be dropped in flight, impairing later combat performance. Thunderbolt pilots could now reach the Dutch-German border, however.

On 30 July, as detailed in Chapter One, the 78th FG demonstrated that the P-47 could now penetrate the airspace over Germany, meet the Luftwaffe head-on over its homeland and emerge from such combat victorious. The rest of 1943 would be spent working out how best to extend that capability as new fighter and bomber groups finally began to join the Eighth Air Force in England.

AGAINST THE ODDS

August 1943 saw an important technical change – fuel pressurisation, which allowed the use of 75-gallon drop tanks that could be carried up to 30,000 ft. Lacking the adverse performance effects associated with the ferry tanks that had previously been used, the new drop tanks allowed P-47s to cover the same range but at more fuel-efficient altitudes.

On 3 August VIII Fighter Command grew from three to four groups when the 353rd FG became operational with its P-47s at Metfield, in Suffolk, the unit flying its first mission six days later.

Additionally, a second group of trained P-47 pilots arrived at Duxford to fill out the ranks. This was Class 43-C, all of whom had received full training in the P-47 from their initial assignment as single-engined pilots. Among them were future aces 2Lts Dick Hewitt and Alwin Juchheim, as well as Ernie Russell – he was the youngest pilot in the 78th, having turned just 19 on 19 May 1943. He had benefited from a policy change following the outbreak of war that allowed an applicant who could demonstrate in tests the knowledge equivalent to two years of college education to enter the service as an Aviation Cadet at the age of 18, which Russell had done upon graduation from high school in Mississippi.

'We were fortunate', Russell recalled, 'to be held off operations for further training at what the group called "Clobber College", where we learned things that we hadn't been taught back in the States, such as how to fly at very high altitudes. We also got in some real instrument time in poor weather, as well as receiving a good indoctrination to German fighter tactics from guys who had learned to fight the hard way'.

In August, VIII Bomber Command began hitting targets deeper in Germany. On the 12th the 78th FG, now being permanently led by Lt Col Stone (with Lt Col Harry Dayhuff as his deputy commander) following the loss of Lt Col McNickle on 30 July, provided escort for raids against the synthetic oil installations at Bochum, Gelsenkirchen and Recklinghausen, in northwestern Germany. Luftwaffe fighters avoided attacking while their USAAF counterparts were present, and the 78th returned to Duxford without incident. Once the P-47s had departed, however, the German fighters attacked the bombers, knocking down 23 and damaging 103, before the 56th FG arrived to escort the survivors back to England.

On 15 August the 78th escorted B-17s targeting Merville, Lille-Vendeville and Vitry-en-Artois airfields in France, but no enemy aircraft were encountered. The following day the 78th provided withdrawal support to B-17s sent to bomb the Renault factory near Le Bourget airfield in Paris. This was the deepest escort mission flown to date, and it was made possible by the new drop tanks. The value of fighter escort was demonstrated when the Luftwaffe chose to oppose this mission, which targeted its main aircraft repair facility in France. With the 4th FG providing support inbound and the 56th FG supplying escorts over the target itself, these two groups claimed 18 Fw 190s and Bf 109s shot down between them.

By the time this photograph of P-47C-5 41-6630 *Spokane Chief* was taken at Duxford in late August 1943, Maj Gene Roberts had claimed six of his eventual nine kills. A close examination of this shot reveals seven swastikas below the fighter's cockpit, which suggests that Roberts was convinced in his own mind that the Fw 190 he claimed as a probable on 1 July 1943 had in fact crashed. By 20 October Roberts had run his score to nine kills, six of them in this very aircraft. Note that 41-6630 has been modified to carry a disposable 75-gallon pressurised drop tank on its centreline (*USAAF*)

17 August saw the Eighth Air Force mount its biggest operation so far when bombers attacked industrial facilities in Regensburg and Schweinfurt. This raid was the USAAF's first attempt to hit truly 'strategic' targets deep in Germany. Five new B-17 groups had become operational over the summer, and all now had sufficient experience to allow VIII Bomber Command to plan and carry out such a major mission. After several cancellations due to adverse weather, Mission 84 was finally set for 17 August 1943 – exactly one year on from the Eighth Air Force's first heavy bomber mission.

The Messerschmitt factory in Regensburg produced half of all Bf 109s built during the war, while Schweinfurt was home to Germany's ball-bearing industry. Col Curtis LeMay's 4th Bombardment Wing (BW) would hit Regensburg while the 1st BW headed for Schweinfurt. Both targets were to be bombed as close to simultaneously as possible so as to split the defending fighters sent to oppose the raids. The Regensburg force would then fly on to North Africa while the 1st BW returned to England. The majority of the mission would be flown beyond the range of fighter escorts.

The Regensburg force was to take off first. Ten minutes after it had crossed the enemy coast the Schweinfurt raiders would depart. Unfortunately, the Eighth Air Force bases in East Anglia were shrouded in fog that morning. Nevertheless, the 4th BW was able to get off at 0800 hrs since LeMay had demanded that his crews become proficient in performing instrument takeoffs. This was not the case for the 1st BW, however, which finally departed at 1330 hrs. Delayed by the poor weather, the wing then had to wait for the P-47 escorts that had returned from the morning operation with the 4th BW to refuel and rearm for the second mission. This deadly gap between strikes allowed the Luftwaffe to attack the 4th BW in force, then land, refuel and rearm, before taking off once again to intercept the 1st BW.

The 4th BW had been targeted by enemy fighters from the time it crossed the Dutch coast, the Luftwaffe calling in aircraft from Holland, Belgium, northern Germany, France, Austria and Italy. Bomber gunners claimed 288 German fighters destroyed – clearly a tally in excess of reality, but a good indicator of the battle's intensity, nevertheless.

Col Beirne Lay Jr, who with Sy Bartlett would later write the classic novel (which became a motion picture) of the Eighth Air Force's war, *Twelve O'Clock High*, flew with the 100th BG on this mission. Called 'the Hambrucken raid' in the novel, Lay remembered, 'After we had been under attack for a solid hour, it appeared our group was faced with annihilation. Seven had been shot down, the sky was still mottled with rising fighters and the target was still 35 minutes away. I doubt if a man in the group visualised the possibility of our getting much further without 100 per cent loss'. The 4th BW had 24 B-17s shot down and 60 damaged from a total force of 146 aircraft – the 100th BG lost nine of the 21 B-17s it sortied.

Maj Gene Roberts leads a mixed formation of 84th FS C- and D-model Thunderbolts in late August 1943. Red-outlined national insignia is in evidence on all the aircraft in this photograph, as are teardrop-shaped 75-gallon belly tanks. Being pressurised, these tanks tended to deliver the specified amount of fuel, unlike the original bulbous tanks that were unpressurised and good for about 100 gallons only. The 75-gallon tanks finally made the P-47 an escort fighter to be reckoned with (*USAAF*)

The 1st BW sent 230 B-17s to strike Schweinfurt. Unfortunately, the 78th FG, which was supposed to relieve the RAF Spitfire escort over Antwerp, in Belgium, arrived eight minutes late due to the adverse weather. The group was immediately engaged by large formations of German fighters and forced to break off after only ten minutes of combat. During this time single victories were claimed by Maj Roberts and Flt Off Pompetti of the 84th FS, the unit having engaged a mixed formation of Bf 110 and 'Me 210' (probably Me 410s) heavy fighters.

By the time the 1st BW arrived at Schweinfurt, 22 of the 57 bombers in the lead formations had been shot down. A further 18 'heavies' were lost before more RAF Spitfires and P-47s from the 353rd and 56th FGs arrived to provide withdrawal support. They claimed 21 German fighters destroyed in the process.

Overall, 60 bombers had been destroyed, with an additional 95 damaged – twice as many B-17s had been lost on 17 August than had previously been downed on a single day. The Luftwaffe had lost 25 fighters in return, with 15 pilots parachuting to safety.

The bombing results at Regensburg were considered excellent, with all six main workshops (including the final assembly plant) at the Messerschmitt factory being either destroyed or severely damaged. Unfortunately, the 500-lb bombs dropped were not powerful enough to destroy the precision machinery within. At Schweinfurt, the two largest factories suffered 80 direct hits and extensive fire damage, but again the ordnance used was not powerful enough to completely destroy the machinery that produced the ball bearings. Despite an immediate 34 per cent loss of production, fighter output was quickly restored, and sufficient ball bearings were found in storage to negate the losses.

This mission epitomised the struggle the Eighth Air Force's bomber groups would face for the rest of 1943 due to VIII Fighter Command's inability to provide deep penetration escort. Losses became so high that the future of the entire daylight bombing campaign was thrown into doubt. As with the reverses that would be suffered during the autumn of 1943, Gen Eaker gave the impression of victory on 17 August when in fact none existed. He wrote postwar;

Capt Charles London formates in his P-47C-2 with a B-17 from the 3rd BD as the bomber heads for Stuttgart on 6 September. This mission proved to be a costly fiasco for the Eighth Air Force as cloud cover frustrated attacks on the briefed targets and formations became separated – a situation enemy defences exploited to the full. A total of 27 B-17s were lost (*USAAF*)

'It was a bold and strategic concept, one of the most significant and remarkable air battles of World War 2. The flight crews demonstrated a determination and courage seldom equalled and never surpassed in warfare. Our bombers could, and did, press through to their assigned targets. This battle resulted in the recall of many squadrons of German fighters from the Eastern Front at a critical time there, in a vain effort to meet the bomber onslaught.'

The truth was that VIII Bomber Command had received such a bloody nose that it was almost three weeks before another deep penetration mission could be mounted.

All four fighter groups provided full escort on 19 August when bombers targeted the airfields at Gilze-Rijen and Flushing, in Belgium. Nine enemy aircraft were shot down, two probably destroyed and four damaged for the loss of one Thunderbolt. 83rd FS pilot Lt K W Dougherty claimed the 78th's solitary victory when he downed a Bf 109 near Woensdrecht airfield, in Holland.

Five days later Maj Gene Roberts became the group's second ace when he destroyed an Fw 190 and a Bf 109 whilst escorting a raid on the air depot at Villacoublay airfield. At 1800 hrs, between Rouen and Evreux, Roberts had attacked two enemy fighters climbing parallel with the bombers at 'one o'clock'. Engaging the Fw 190 first, he registered many hits before breaking off to avoid colliding with his opponent. The fighter burst into flames and spun away. Roberts then went after the Bf 109, which was seen to trail smoke before exploding.

On 27 August all four fighter groups sent 178 P-47s to escort the first bombing mission against a V1 launch site, which was under construction at Watten, in the Nord-Pas-de-Calais region of France. Eight Fw 190s were shot down, but none were credited to the 78th.

An abortive mission on 2 September saw 233 B-17s sent to attack airfields in northern France, only to be recalled due to bad weather. Missions over northern France were successfully flown on 3 and 4 September, however, although the 78th again saw no opposition.

On 6 September VIII Bomber Command sent 400 'heavies' to target the VKF ball-bearing factory in Stuttgart, Germany. Some 176 P-47s from all four groups provided escort inbound and outbound, but German fighters refused to engage – one Fw 190 was claimed for the loss of a single P-47. Once the escorts left, however, the Luftwaffe succeeded in downing 45 bombers – more than ten per cent of the attacking force. Such losses were unsustainable.

The Luftwaffe failed to rise to the bait of USAAF bombers with fighter escorts over the Low Countries and northern France on 7, 8 and 9 September. While it may seem surprising that fighter pilots from VIII Fighter Command would not meet their German counterparts on

almost every mission, as they had in June and July, the *Jagdgeschwadern* had reverted to the strategy used during the RAF's 'Non-Stop Offensive' in 1941 – the defenders did not rise to every challenge. This was particularly the case with long distance missions, as waiting until the escorts departed gave the defenders a huge advantage.

Additionally, the escort policy implemented by VIII Fighter Command at the time limited opportunities to fight. The P-47 pilots' primary mission was to provide vulnerable bombers with close escort, and fighter groups were ordered not to go after German formations even when they were forming up for attack. Aggressive pilots like Peter Pompetti, who disregarded formation integrity to chase German aircraft, could, and did, find themselves removed from operations following repeated offences.

This was due in part to the continuing belief that the Thunderbolt was too unwieldy to successfully take on a German single-seater in a turning fight, despite the fighter groups' impressive record during the summer months of 1943. It was also feared that greater aggression would draw the escorts away, leaving the bombers open to attack by additional enemy aircraft. Dogfighting with German aircraft used up the P-47s' precious supply of fuel far more rapidly, making an early withdrawal necessary. Finally, there were not enough fighters to provide such an aggressive escort.

The problems associated with the P-47's modest range eased a little from 27 September, when the 78th FG made use of new 108-gallon paper drop tanks for the first time. With each Thunderbolt carrying a single tank on its centreline, the additional fuel meant that pilots could fly 200 miles into Germany and still have ten minutes' fuel remaining for combat. That day, 45 Thunderbolts led by Lt Col Dayhuff headed for the rendezvous point ten miles west of Emden, in northwestern Germany. Dayhuff was leading the 83rd FS at 27,000 ft, with the 84th at 29,000 ft

A Thunderbolt from the 82nd FS flies close escort to B-17s of the 94th BG during the raid on Emden on 27 September 1943. Despite the 78th FG downing nine German fighters during this mission, seven B-17s were still lost – three of them from the 94th BG (*USAAF*)

Capt John Irvin of the 84th FS was amongst the victorious pilots on 27 September 1943, claiming a Bf 109 destroyed north of Emden. This proved to be his final success, having previously claimed an Fw 190 on 16 May and another Focke-Wulf fighter and a Bf 109 on 30 July. His P-47C-5 41-6367 *Geronimo* was originally named *Unmentionable*. Irvin, who had joined the 84th in May 1942, served as the unit's operations officer until he completed his tour in March 1944. The broom symbols to the left of the crew panel on this machine denoted how many fighter sweeps the P-47 had participated in, whilst brooms with bombs symbolised bomber support missions. Such markings were religiously applied to all early Thunderbolts assigned to the 78th FG, but this tradition died out during early 1944 (*USAAF*)

and the high-cover 82nd at 32,000 ft. As they approached Emden, the P-47 pilots spotted 30 Bf 109s making rocket-firing passes at the heavy bombers – two of which were seen to fall away from the formation engulfed in flames. The Luftwaffe had no expectation of meeting American fighters this far north, and the 78th hit them hard.

83rd FS CO Maj J C Davis and squadronmate Lt Everett Powell each sent a rocket-carrying Bf 109 spinning down in flames, as did Capts Harold Stump and John Irvin and Lt Peter Pompetti of the 84th. The latter also despatched a Bf 110, the aircraft spiralling earthwards after its pilot had been left incapacitated. Minutes later Maj Gene Roberts and his element leader, Lt Quince Brown, closed on a pair of Bf 109s. Roberts could not get into a good firing position on the lead Messerschmitt, but Brown set the wingman on fire to claim his first kill. At this point the high cover 82nd FS dove into the fight, allowing unit CO and future ace Maj Jack Oberhansly to down a Bf 109 and claim a second one as a probable. Squadronmate Flt Off Manuel Martinez was also credited with a Bf 109 destroyed.

With the German attack swiftly broken up during the course of a five-minute fight, the Thunderbolts regrouped and stayed with the bombers, beating off further attempted interceptions until fuel forced them to leave 40 miles off the Dutch coast. The Thunderbolt pilots landed at the first airfields they could find, rather than pressing on to Duxford.

The 78th was the day's top-scoring group, with nine destroyed (and two probables) for no losses out of an overall VIII Fighter Command claim of 21 enemy aircraft destroyed for just one loss. These results clearly demonstrated what was possible when USAAF fighters were able to engage the Luftwaffe, instead of rigidly escorting the bombers. This mission proved to be Lt Col Harry Dayhuff's last with the 78th, as he left shortly thereafter to take up a staff position within VIII Fighter Command. Leading group ace Gene Roberts replaced Dayhuff as deputy commander, while Maj Jack Price took command of the 84th FS.

September ended with claims of nine destroyed by group pilots during 14 missions, for the loss of just one pilot killed in action. An added benefit of the new drop tanks was that it gave fighter groups the ability to retrace the escort route more than once, thus allowing P-47s to come to the aid of damaged bombers straggling behind the main formations that had heretofore been easy kills for German aircraft.

Despite the successes of September, VIII Bomber Command continued to suffer terrible losses to the Luftwaffe in October. For example, on the 10th, during a deep penetration mission to targets in Anklam and Marienburg, 28 bombers were shot down – eight per cent of the attacking force. An additional 30 were downed the next day over Münster – 13 per cent of the attacking force. Such attrition was unsustainable.

The 78th FG had encountered enemy fighters for the first time in a fortnight whilst escorting bombers as they departed Münster. The group intercepted 15 Bf 110s and Me 410s, along with 18 Bf 109s, when they attacked a straggling formation of B-17s. Gene Roberts bounced a Bf 110, setting an engine afire. Rolling away to avoid the resulting explosion, he then attacked a Me 410, closing to point-blank range before it too exploded – pieces from the shattered Messerschmitt damaged the Thunderbolt of wingman Glenn Koontz. Roberts' score of eight now made him the top ace in VIII Fighter Command. 84th FS pilots Lt C W Silsby and P L Larson, also enjoyed success, the former downing a Bf 110 and an 'Me 210' and the latter a Bf 110. Overall, the 216 P-47 pilots from the five groups escorting this mission claimed 19 enemy fighters destroyed for the loss of one Thunderbolt.

Bad weather kept the 78th grounded on 14 October, when VIII Bomber Command returned to Schweinfurt on the mission that became known as 'Black Thursday'. No fewer than 60 bombers were shot down over Germany and more than 100 badly damaged of the 290 sent out. The Luftwaffe had inflicted a defeat so stunning that it led to a complete change in strategy. In the two months since the first Schweinfurt mission on 17 August, 148 B-17s and B-24s had been lost – nearly 40 per cent of all heavy bombers in England. Many more were so badly damaged that they were scrapped. On 15 October VIII Bomber Command could not have mustered 100 bombers. At this point in the campaign, statistically, there was no chance of a bomber crewman surviving a 25-mission tour. Indeed, a man flying his sixth mission was effectively living on someone else's time.

The theory of self-defending bomber formations flying missions without fighter escort had been shot down in flames over Schweinfurt. Only the fact that the weather closed in for the next two months, preventing any deep penetration missions being flown until mid-December, allowed the Eighth Air Force to hide the magnitude of its defeat. On 15 October the first of two long-range P-38 groups, the 55th FG, flew its first sweep over northern France. It was a very dim light in a very dark tunnel.

Five days later Lt Col Gene Roberts claimed his ninth, and last, victory whilst escorting bombers sent to attack industrial plants in Düren, Germany. The Bf 109 he downed over Dinant, in Belgium, was the 78th's sole victory on this date. Another Bf 109 was shared by 82nd FS pilots Capt W E May and Lt A W Hill on 24 October when the 78th supplied aircraft to escort B-26s of the Ninth Air Force attacking targets in northern Normandy.

Another kill is added to the 84th FS's victory board at Duxford in October 1943. By war's end the unit had claimed 93.5 aerial victories – the lowest tally of the three squadrons in the group. Conversely, it had been credited with 113 strafing kills – the highest tally in the 78th (*USAAF*)

The third pilot to 'make ace' in the 78th FG was Capt Jack Price of the 84th FS, who achieved this feat on 26 November 1943. He became squadron CO when Gene Roberts was moved up to group staff. Price is seen here in P-47C-2 41-6270 *Feather Merchant*, in which he claimed his first victory (an Fw 190 near Abbeville, France) on 14 July 1943. He completed his tour with the 84th FS in February 1944, but returned to the ETO in October of that year and saw further action – although he claimed no further kills – with the 20th FG (*USAAF*)

The group's next successes came on 3 November, during a raid that marked the first step in the operational recovery of the Eighth Air Force. Some 539 bombers were sent to attack the German port city of Wilhemshaven, with target escort being provided by the 55th FG, which enjoyed some success. Additionally, 11 B-17 Pathfinders equipped with H2X (the American equivalent of British H2S) radar marked the target – it became the first to be completely destroyed by blind bombing. A total of 333 P-47s (including fighters from the 78th) also provided escort all the way to and from the target, and 82nd FS pilot Lt C B Hahn claimed a Bf 109 destroyed.

With P-47s now pouring into England, units were able to double their establishment and fly 'A' and 'B' group missions of 36 aircraft each. This was first done by the 78th on 5 November, when VIII Bomber Command returned to Gelsenkirchen and Münster. Group commander Col Stone duly led group 78A while deputy group commander Lt Col Roberts headed group 78B.

Bad weather adversely affected mission effectiveness for much of November, and it was not until the 26th that the 78th FG encountered German aircraft once again. By then the P-38 had become firmly established within VIII Fighter Command, despite a number of examples from the 55th FG being lost to engine failure at high altitude. These mechanical problems aside, the Lightning offered a substantial range advantage over the P-47, and it would be heavily utilised for target escort in the coming battles over Germany.

Technological change arrived for the Thunderbolt-equipped groups during November. Republic had redesigned the P-47 so that it could carry a 108-gallon drop tank on a rack beneath each wing, in addition to the centreline tank. New aeroplanes arrived in England already equipped, while VIII Service Command modified frontline fighters in the field. When the weather finally broke in December, the Thunderbolt's lack of range had been resolved.

On 26 November the 78th's A and B group missions were flown to Montdidier, in France, where 30 Fw 190s were intercepted. 84th FS CO Maj Jack Price 'made ace' with his fourth and fifth victories (an Fw 190 and a Bf 109, the latter exploding in flames) near Paris. Squadronmate Lt Howard Askelson downed one of three Bf 109s attacking a B-17, while Lt Warren Wessell of the 82nd FS destroyed an Fw 190 from a distance of 600 yards. These proved to be hard won victories, however, as each squadron lost an aircraft, resulting in one pilot being killed and two captured.

Four days later Maj Jack Oberhansly led 78B Group to Aachen, in Germany, supporting bombers attacking industrial sites in nearby Solingen. Barrelling in behind an Fw 190, he had to pull up and correctly identify the target when someone called it out as a P-47 over the radio.

Ensuring it was indeed a German fighter, Oberhansly rolled back in astern of his foe and shot it down for his second kill. That same day, the 78A Group mission, led by Gene Roberts, was cancelled by poor weather just as the fighters were crossing the Channel. Requesting homing back to Duxford, the 36 Thunderbolts finally broke out of thick cloud directly over London's balloon barrage 50 miles south of

Future ace Maj Jack Oberhansly guns the engine of his fighter, P-47D-2 42-7883 *IRON ASS*, at Duxford in late 1943. This was his second Thunderbolt, and he claimed two victories (a Bf 109 on 27 September and an Fw 190 on 30 November 1943) and a probable (a Bf 109 on 27 September) in it. The aircraft is carrying a 100-lb bomb rather than a drop tank on this occasion (*USAAF*)

Duxford! Bad weather throughout November had seen the 78th fly only 11 missions, claiming six victories for three losses.

On 1 December the group celebrated its first year in the ETO with an escort to Duren. Over nearby Eupen, in Belgium, future ace Lt James Wilkinson of the 82nd FS claimed his first victory when he destroyed a Bf 109. Minutes later, 84th FS pilot Lt Charles Keppler sent down an Fw 190 over Liège-Aachen.

The return of poor weather then prevented further missions being flown for the next ten days, the 78th using this break in operations to master the art of dive-bombing in the P-47.

Improving conditions allowed Lt G W Koontz of the 84th FS to down a Bf 109 on 11 December, and future ace Lt H T Barnaby of the 83rd FS repeated this success with a Messerschmitt nine days later. A third Bf 109 fell to squadronmate Lt M D Putnam on 22 December, all three of these victories being claimed during bomber escorts to Germany.

Gene Roberts, who remained the group's ranking ace with nine victories, had been pulled off operations on 18 December and sent to join Harry Dayhuff at VIII Fighter Command as an operational 'troubleshooter'.

The year's last escort, on 30 December, saw 78A Group provide withdrawal support near Saint Mihiel, in France, where future ace Lt William Julian of the 83rd FS scored his first victory – a Bf 109 that he caught sneaking up on a straggler. 82nd FS pilots Lts Warren Wesson (also a future ace), Manuel Martinez and William Hegman also destroyed a Bf 109 apiece.

The 78th flew its first dive-bombing mission on 31 December, closing out the momentous year of 1943 with an attack on Gilze-Rijen airfield. The group also sent aircraft on an escort mission for bombers targeting French airfields, and Lt Julian doubled his score with an Fw 190 destroyed near Lorient. Squadronmate Lt H C Roff also downed a Focke-Wulf.

The 78th FG had flown nine missions in December and claimed eleven victories for two losses. Overall, the group had completed 113 missions in 1943, claiming 71 enemy aircraft destroyed, 13 probables and 27 damaged for 29 losses.

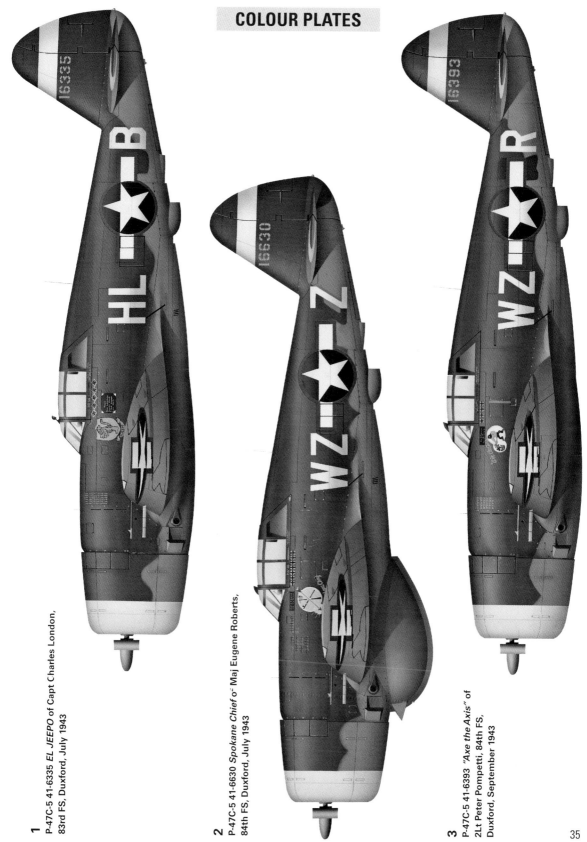

1
P-47C-5 41-6335 *EL JEEPO* of Capt Charles London,
83rd FS, Duxford, July 1943

2
P-47C-5 41-6630 *Spokane Chief* of Maj Eugene Roberts,
84th FS, Duxford, July 1943

3
P-47C-5 41-6393 *"Axe the Axis"* of
2Lt Peter Pompetti, 84th FS,
Duxford, September 1943

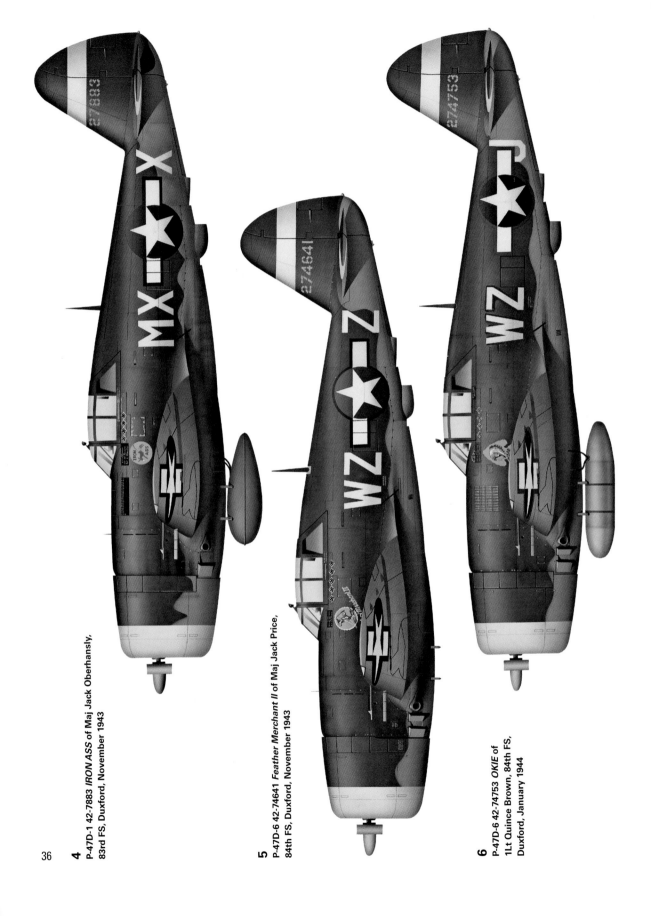

4

P-47D-1 42-7883 *IRON ASS* of Maj Jack Oberhansly,
83rd FS, Duxford, November 1943

5

P-47D-6 42-74641 *Feather Merchant II* of Maj Jack Price,
84th FS, Duxford, November 1943

6

P-47D-6 42-74753 *OKIE* of
1Lt Quince Brown, 84th FS,
Duxford, January 1944

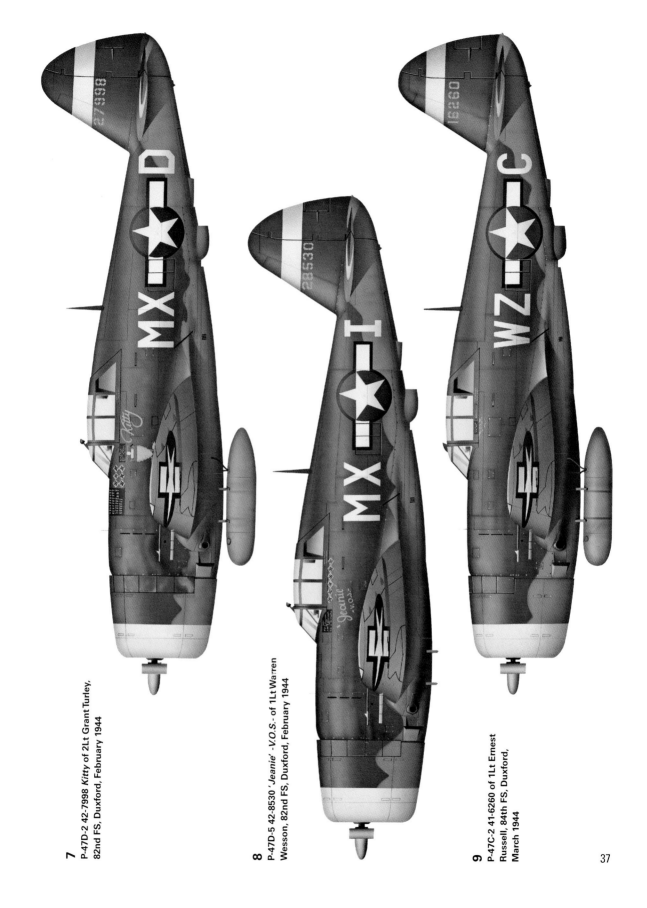

7
P-47D-2 42-7998 *Kitty* of 2Lt Grant Turley,
82nd FS, Duxford, February 1944

8
P-47D-5 42-8530 '*Jeanie*' *- V.O.S.-* of 1Lt Warren
Wesson, 82nd FS, Duxford, February 1944

9
P-47C-2 41-6260 of 1Lt Ernest
Russell, 84th FS, Duxford,
March 1944

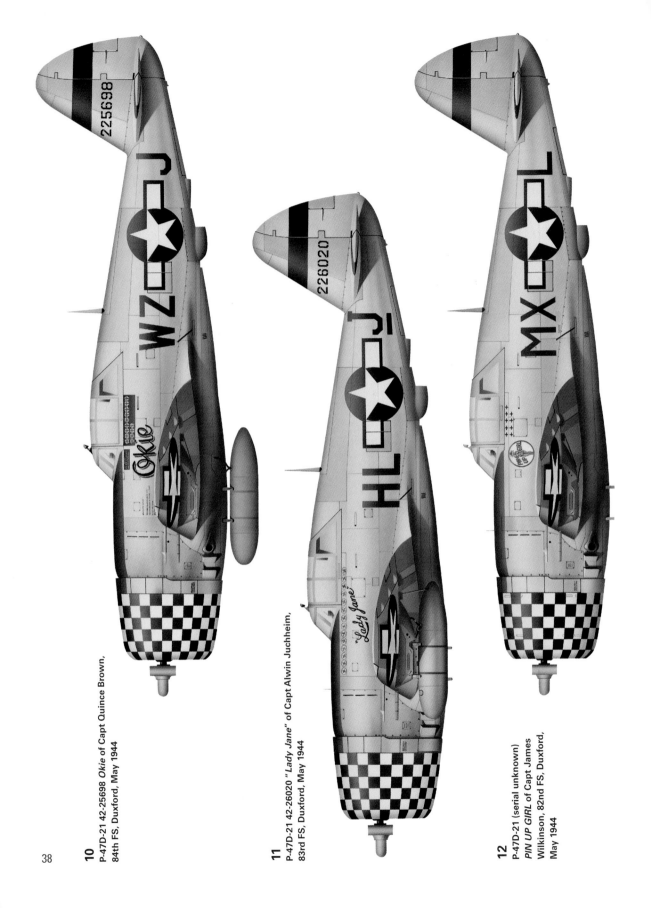

10
P-47D-21 42-25698 *Okie* of Capt Quince Brown,
84th FS, Duxford, May 1944

11
P-47D-21 42-26020 *"Lady Jane"* of Capt Alwin Juchheim,
83rd FS, Duxford, May 1944

12
P-47D-21 (serial unknown)
PIN UP GIRL of Capt James
Wilkinson, 82nd FS, Duxford,
May 1944

13

P-47D-25 42-26671 *No Guts – No Glory!* of Capt Ben Mayo,
82nd FS, Duxford, June 1944

14

P-47D-25 42-27339 of Maj Joseph Myers, 82nd FS,
Duxford, September 1944

15

P-47D-28 42-28878 *Eileen* of
1Lt Frank Oiler, 84th FS,
Duxford, September 1944

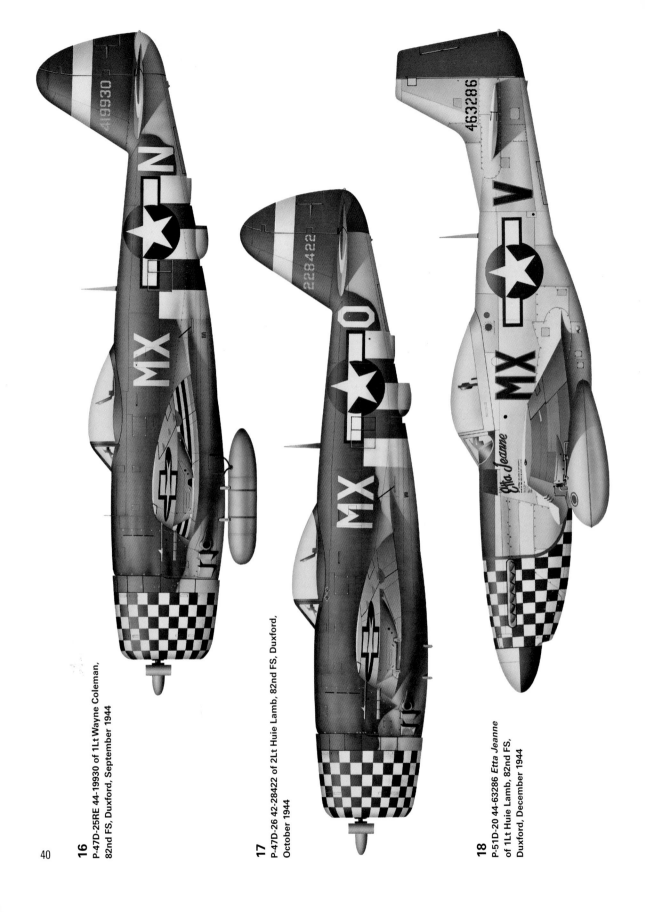

16
P-47D-25RE 44-19930 of 1Lt Wayne Coleman,
82nd FS, Duxford, September 1944

17
P-47D-26 42-28422 of 2Lt Huie Lamb, 82nd FS, Duxford,
October 1944

18
P-51D-20 44-63286 *Etta Jeanne*
of 1Lt Huie Lamb, 82nd FS,
Duxford, December 1944

19
P-51D-20 44-63209 *Sherman was Right!* of 1Lt Frank Oiler,
84th FS, Duxford, January 1945

20
P-51D-20 44-63712 *FLY'N TIME EOMB* of Maj Ray
Smith, 84th FS, Duxford, February 1945

21
P-51D-20 44-63187 *Bum Steer*
of 1Lt Earl Stier, 84th FS,
Duxford, February 1945

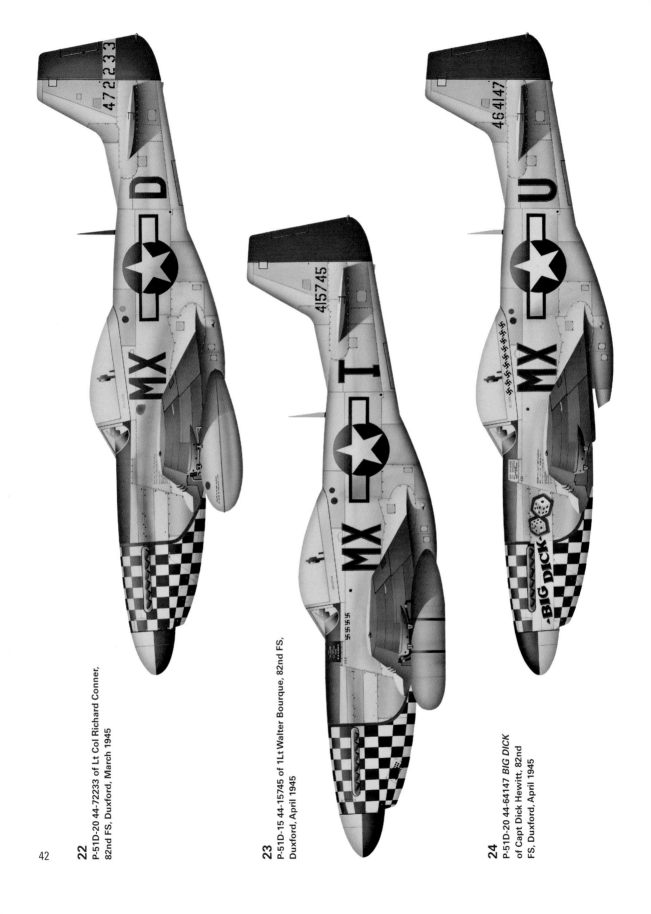

22
P-51D-20 44-72233 of Lt Col Richard Conner,
82nd FS, Duxford, March 1945

23
P-51D-15 44-15745 of 1Lt Walter Bourque, 82nd FS,
Duxford, April 1945

24
P-51D-20 44-64147 *BIG DICK*
of Capt Dick Hewitt, 82nd
FS, Duxford, April 1945

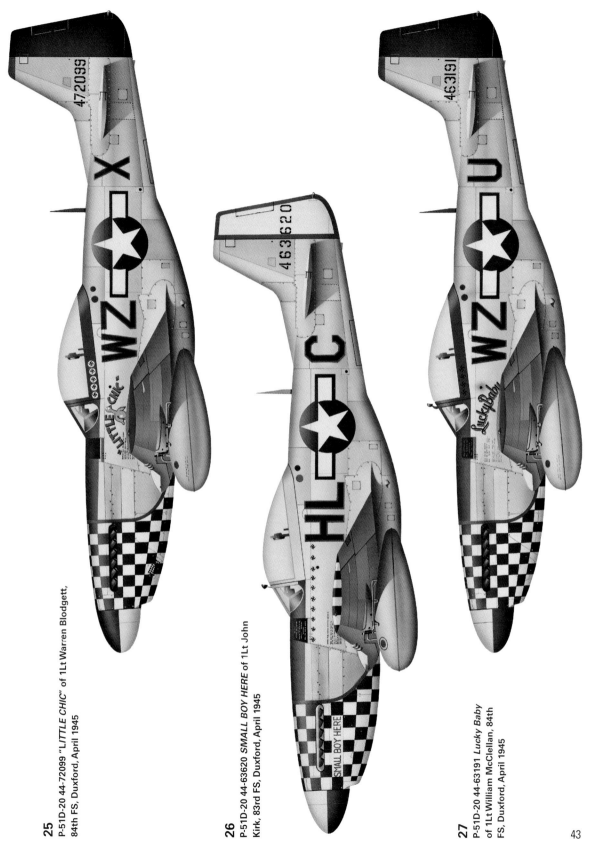

25

P-51D-20 44-72099 "*LITTLE CHIC*" of 1Lt Warren Blodgett, 84th FS, Duxford, April 1945

26

P-51D-20 44-63620 *SMALL BOY HERE* of 1Lt John Kirk, 83rd FS, Duxford, April 1945

27

P-51D-20 44-63191 *Lucky Baby* of 1Lt William McClellan, 84th FS, Duxford, April 1945

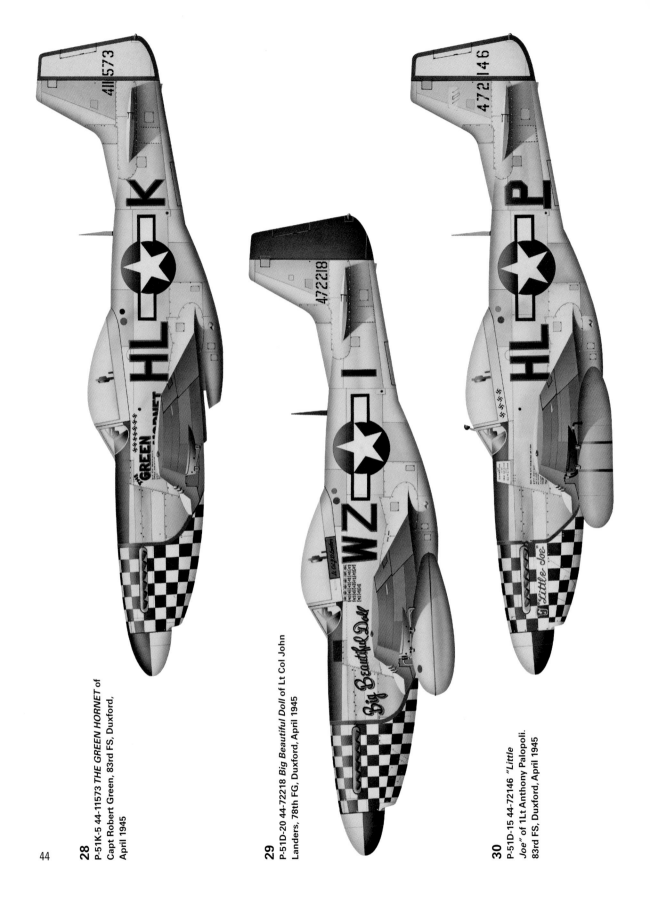

44

28
P-51K-5 44-11573 *THE GREEN HORNET* of Capt Robert Green, 83rd FS, Duxford, April 1945

29
P-51D-20 44-72218 *Big Beautiful Doll* of Lt Col John Landers, 78th FG, Duxford, April 1945

30
P-51D-15 44-72146 *"Little Joe"* of 1Lt Anthony Palopoli. 83rd FS, Duxford, April 1945

BATTLE OF GERMANY

New Year's Day brought the certainty that 1944 would be the war's decisive year. During the Quebec Conference of August 1943 a date had been set for a cross-Channel invasion – 1 May 1944. For the Eighth Air Force, the pressure was on. The defeat of the Luftwaffe was the goal without which there could be no successful invasion of occupied Europe.

As of 1 January, the Eighth Air Force was some way off achieving that goal. The Luftwaffe was far from being a spent force, with aircraft production being increased monthly and the output of replacement pilots keeping pace with losses – admittedly, the *'Nachwuchs'* ('new growth') *jagdflieger* did not have the same level of training that had been standard just a year earlier. Nevertheless, the *Jagdgeschwadern* were confident of their ability to make their American counterparts pay so heavy a price in the skies over Germany that the daylight aerial bombing campaign would have to be abandoned.

For the USAAF, the power of sheer numbers would be the key to victory. The call for the training of 50,000 pilots annually issued in 1941 was fulfilled. Replacements with a minimum of 400 hours of training were now filling the veteran groups of the Eighth Air Force to bursting, turning each group effectively into two, while new units arrived each month. In January 1944 Lt Gen Ira Eaker was sent to command the newly created Fifteenth Air Force in Italy, his position at the head of the Eighth Air Force being taken by Lt Gen Jimmy Doolittle. America's premier pilot, Doolittle could claim personal responsibility for the fact that Allied air forces ran on 100-octane aviation gasoline from his days with Shell Oil, when he championed its development. His personal example as leader of the Tokyo Raid in April 1942 set him apart from all other USAAF commanders.

The coming duel could be called the Battle of Germany as surely as the German attempt to set the stage for an invasion in 1940 was called the Battle of Britain. With a forecast for better weather in February, Doolittle ordered the commencement of the daylight campaign. After poor conditions during the first two weeks of the month prevented missions into Germany, an extensive high pressure system arrived over northern Europe on 19 February, promising the first extended period of good visibility since the previous autumn. What came to be called 'Big Week' was a series of major strikes against the German aircraft industry throughout the rest of the month.

For the fighters, two changes in strategy and tactics instigated in January 1944 would have a major effect in the coming battles. Shortly after assuming command, Doolittle announced he would 'turn the fighters loose'. This order resulted in several fighter groups running up their scores in the next few months as the daylight offensive hit its stride. However, the change was not universally adopted. Some group commanders disagreed with the new strategy, maintaining the close escort policy that had been observed for more than a year. Prominent among these was Col Stone, with the end result that the 78th FG would not score anywhere near as many victories as the 4th or 56th FGs, despite having served alongside them from the very beginning of the campaign in the ETO.

Doolittle made one other change. With the Luftwaffe increasingly avoiding combat as more USAAF fighters appeared in the skies of western Europe, the only place their aircraft could be found was on their airfields. Any fighter group that had finished its escort assignment without engaging the enemy, and had sufficient fuel remaining, was to find and hit German airfields on their return leg home.

Strafing changed the rules. A fighter-versus-fighter engagement was a test of skill and ability. Low-level attack was a question of whether one could survive the laws of probability. German airfields bristled with a multitude of anti-aircraft artillery, from 88 mm high altitude guns through 50 mm and 37 mm medium altitude weapons to rapidly-firing 20 mm cannon for use against low-level strafers, all of which threw up a veritable wall of fire that an attacking fighter had to fly through. The odds were against the strafer, even in a fast aeroplane that could take hits and keep going like the Thunderbolt.

To counter the initial reluctance of pilots to engage in strafing, Doolittle ruled that a 'ground kill' – the successful destruction of an aircraft by strafing – would be viewed in the same way as an aerial victory. No other Army Air Force in any theatre adopted such a policy. The result was that more than two-thirds of the German aircraft claimed destroyed between 'Big Week' and D-Day were strafing victories, while 70 per cent of VIII Fighter Command losses were from such missions.

Tactics were not the only determinant of a group's success. Mission assignments were also crucial, with a group assigned to the leading formation being more likely to find enemy fighters than one in the rear. As squadron commanders completed their tours, some group COs (like 'Hub' Zemke of the 56th FG) did what they could to have one or more of these veteran aviators transferred to VIII Fighter Command Operations, where mission assignments were made. This was done by transferring said individuals from combat operations to VIII Fighter Command staff *before* their tour expired, thus keeping them under the same operational commander. The 78th FG found itself at a disadvantage, since Gene Roberts and Harry Dayhuff were in tactical development at VIII Fighter Command rather than in the operation planning section, bringing new groups into combat.

Additionally, Duxford was 50 miles further west than the next VIII Fighter Command base in East Anglia. This in turn meant that the 78th could not get target support assignments – where the chance of combat was greatest – due to the group's relative lack of range in comparison with the 56th, based near the coast at Halesworth, or the 4th, only 30 miles inland at Debden. This geographical difficulty and the 'politics' of VIII Fighter Command would remain a bone of contention among pilots of the 78th FG for the rest of the war, and would be remembered long after VE Day.

Nevertheless, the group celebrated New Year with a bang, literally. Flying withdrawal support for the 3rd Bomb Division's mission to Münster on 4 January, the 83rd FS's 'Yellow Flight' (part of 78A Group) dove from 26,000 ft down to 15,000 ft to bounce five Fw 190s. Lt Harry Rolf recalled;

A He 111 erupts under the fire of eight 0.50-in machine guns as Lt James Wilkinson strafes a German airfield near Paris on 6 February 1944. The future eight-victory ace was credited with damaging two Heinkel bombers, having earlier shot down an Fw 190 over Orléans-Bricy. The 78th had attacked four airfields in accordance with Lt Gen Doolittle's new orders, which had been issued earlier that same day to VIII Fighter Command. He had tasked its units with strafing airfields after they had escorted bombers targeting similar sites in France (*USAAF*)

P-47C/Ds from the 82nd FS await their next sorties from Duxford on 7 February 1944. Note the individual nature of the horizontal stripes applied to each machine, and also the off-white colour of the squadron codes. The fighter third from the camera, P-47D-2 42-7954, was assigned to Lt James Wilkinson. He used it to claim his first victory (a Bf 109) on 1 December 1943, and possibly the Fw 190 he downed on 6 February 1944. Parked next to it is Capt Bob Eby's P-47C-2 41-6249 *Vee Gail*

'We missed in the first pass and I then rolled in on a Focke-Wulf that overshot me, and chased him down to 12,000 ft, firing all the time. His canopy finally came off, and he came out with his 'chute opening very quickly.'

Squadronmate Lt J E Stokes also destroyed an Fw 190.

Lt Quince Brown, leading the 84th FS's 'Bayland Blue Flight', brought his four fighters down on 12 Fw 190s, closing to 50 yards and sending one spinning away. Making a sharp right turn, he hit a second with a 30-degrees deflection shot, setting it aflame. While Brown was busy, squadronmate Lt Peter Pompetti dove on two radial-engined fighters that turned out to be P-47s. Continuing in his dive, he then saw 16 Bf 109s attacking a straggler over Coesfeld, west of Münster. Closing in a near-vertical dive, he hit one fighter with a burst that lasted from 50 yards down to just five, before he pushed into a negative-g bunt to miss the enemy fighter by inches as it caught fire, with parts of the Bf 109 hitting his wing. This success gave Pompetti ace status.

On the return leg of the mission, Lt James Wilkinson of the 82nd FS claimed the group's first locomotive victory when he strafed a train near Dorsten, in Germany. Squadronmate Lt 'Manny' Martinez, escorting a wingman in his damaged fighter, was chased by four Bf 109s that forced them into the clouds over Antwerp. Emerging from the overcast at low altitude, Martinez spotted a Bf 109 with its wheels down preparing to land. He immediately shot it out of the sky, and then strafed the airfield the Messerschmitt was attempting to land at. Martinez duly made the group's first strafing claim when he set a Bf 110 alight.

The next day (5th), 78B Group was given the unenviable task of staying with the bombers from the 3rd BD as they headed back from bombing Bordeaux-Mérignac airfield, in France. Left waiting for their relief to arrive, the P-47 pilots found themselves extremely low on fuel when they were bounced by Fw 190s that appeared out of thick haze. Having reduced their speed so as to extend their range, the Thunderbolt pilots struggled to defend themselves. Five P-47s were quickly shot down, with four pilots killed and one captured. Earlier in the mission Lts Quince Brown and Philip Larson had each downed a Bf 109 over La Rochelle.

The onset of bad weather allowed the 78th to make good the losses it suffered on 5 January – the heaviest since it became operational eight months earlier. Two more pilots were killed on the 24th, when German fighters were encountered once again, although this time their loss was blamed on fuel starvation – the 82nd FS machines crashed into the Channel. The group had claimed two victories that day, one of these (a Bf 110) falling to future ace Lt John Hockery of the 82nd FS.

Continuing poor weather restricted operations to northern France and Belgium. On 25 January Col Stone led the first 'Thunderbomber' mission to Walcheren Island, where the weather was so bad that the group could see no targets and duly brought the bombs home.

Conditions improved sufficiently on the 29th for Lt Col Dayhuff to take 78B Group to Koblenz as withdrawal support for bombers attacking Frankfurt, where three Fw 190s were downed. The following day Lt Quince Brown attacked an aeroplane over Rheine, in Germany, that he initially misidentified as a P-51 (examples of the Packard-Merlin-engined fighter had begun arriving in the ETO in late 1943). He quickly realised his mistake, rolled in and shot down the Bf 109 to 'make ace'. 31 January saw the group's first successful dive-bombing mission of 1944 when the 82nd FS and half of the 83rd FS as 78A Group, led by Maj Oberhansly, dropped 35 500-lb bombs on Gilze-Rijen airfield, while 78B Group provided top cover. The 78th had managed 12 missions in January, despite bad weather, and had claimed a new record of 14 victories for the loss of eight P-47s.

2Lt Grant Turley seated in P-47D-2 42-7998 *Kitty/SUNDOWN RANCH* with his crew (from left to right), armourer James Sterner, crew chief Alfred Torrow and assistant crew chief Albert Costelnick. Turley scored his first victories (after 14 missions without ever seeing a German) on 10 February 1944 and his sixth just two weeks later. On 6 March 1944 he chased several Fw 190s down to low level in this aircraft, where he got into a turning fight with three more Focke-Wulfs and scored his seventh victory (which was never confirmed) before being shot down moments later (*Robert F Dorr Collection*)

On 6 February, in accordance with Lt Gen Doolittle's new orders, VIII Fighter Command tasked its units with strafing airfields after they had escorted bombers targeting similar sites in France. After chasing Fw 190s (single examples of which were shot down by Lts Warren Wesson and James Wilkinson) at low-level during an escort to Troyes, in France, 78A Group's pilots were introduced to the many light flak guns around airfields at Orléans-Bricy, Beaumont, Chartres and Evreux. Two days later airfields near Paris were targeted, and Lt Wesson claimed two Heinkel bombers destroyed.

It was quickly discovered that attacking airfields without a plan was a recipe for disaster, however, prompting 'Hub' Zemke to circulate his carefully crafted strafing guide. Airfields spotted whilst returning from an escort mission were put on a list for future action, rather than an immediate strike. Having been briefed on the airfield prior to attacking it, the group would approach the target at low level before dropping to treetop height, line abreast, and making one wide pass. Pilots were urged to stay low for a further five miles before pulling up so as to be certain that they were out of flak range. When a target was too juicy to pass up on first sight, the rule was to fly past it as though it had been unspotted, drop down 20 miles away and return for a single pass. Anything else was certain to result in increased casualties due to flak batteries being at full alert.

Col Stone led 78A Group to Meppel on 10 February, where they caught 40 German fighters preparing to attack the rear bombers of the lead box bound for targets in Brunswick, Germany. Future ace 2Lt Grant Turley of the 82nd FS had not seen an enemy machine in 14 previous missions, but he made up for it now. Writing to his parents, he reported;

'Took off this morning for just an ordinary escort mission, but it turned out I got two Me 109s. We were bounced at 26,000 ft by these jokers. Yours truly and his wingman got on their tails and followed them down. When the leader levelled off on the deck, I got in a burst and he blew up and went in from 300 ft. Looked like one big splash of flame when he hit. I then got on the tail of the second one and he crash-landed in flames.

1Lt Gerald E Brasher of the 82nd FS scored his single aerial victory on 11 February 1944 when he chased down a Bf 109 using his fighter's new water-injection system during an escort to Verdun. He also claimed five strafing victories, four of them shared before completing his 65-mission tour in May 1944 (*USAAF*)

1Lt Alwin Juchheim, who was the 83rd FS's ranking ace, has a last minute conversation with his crew chief prior to climbing into P-47D-6 42-74690 in February 1944. Juchheim claimed five of his nine aerial victories and four of his six strafing kills in this aircraft, which appears to be bereft of any personal markings (*USAAF*)

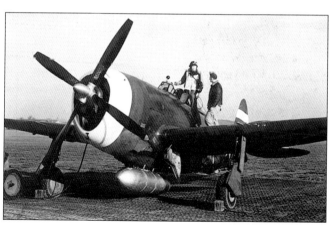

The only losses were Jones and Ludwig [both of whom were killed], my roommates. So it is, one never knows who will be next. Right now it worries me that I have murdered one man and probably another. I guess I'll get callous. However, it is nice to say "planes destroyed" and not think of the pilots.'

Aside from Turley's success, squadronmates Lts W M Wesson and V Y Jones were also credited with victories, although the latter was shot down and killed moments later. 83rd FS pilots claimed five fighters destroyed, with future ace Lt Harold Barnaby getting two of them. The 82nd FS downed four more fighters the following day, with all of them being credited to future aces Lts Hockery, Brasher and Turley, who again scored a brace of kills.

20 February saw the start of 'Big Week', and the 78th was heavily engaged that day. Again, future aces of the 82nd FS dominated the scoring, with Lts Hockery, Wilkinson and Turley all claiming fighters over Koblenz. Indeed, the Fw 190 credited to Turley gave him ace status, as he noted in a letter to his parents;

'Bad weather all week, no flying till today. Eight Fw 190s were encountered over Belgium. Yours truly got one, bringing his total to five. Well, I'm an ace now. It is a thrill and yet not nearly as much as I thought it would be. Sometimes I wish that we didn't have them outnumbered so badly. But in war you can't let your feelings get the upper hand. After all, it is he or you!'

Maj Oberhansly led 78A Group on 22 February to Cologne, where they found bombers were under attack from 40 Bf 109s and Fw 190s. Spotting the escorts, the Germans dove away, followed by the Thunderbolts. In a fight that went from 22,000 ft down to the deck, Oberhansly destroyed a Bf 109 and an Fw 190, while future ace Lt Alwin Juchheim nailed a Messerschmitt as his first kill. Capt Kenneth Dougherty chased four to the deck, losing his wingman in the process, and then discovered another four on his tail. Firing at the lead pair while jinking to avoid the others, he set one afire. Pushing the throttle into war emergency and pulling away to safety, Dougherty praised the new water injection system and paddle blade propellors fitted to his P-47 on returning to Duxford Three more Fw 190s were claimed by the 83rd FS before the unit broke off the fight.

Coming back out of Germany, Oberhansly caught a damaged Fw 190 near Gilze-Rijen airfield and shot it down. This victory made him an ace. A few minutes later, as Oberhansly and his wingman prepared to turn into two

Crew chief TSgt Clarence Koskela
paints a sixth swastika on P-47D-5
42-8530 'Jeanie' -V.O.S.- as pilot
1Lt Warren Wesson watches – Jean
was Wesson's wife and V.O.S.
was an acronym for 'Victory Over
Separation'. Wesson, serving with the
82nd FS, claimed four aerial and two
strafing kills between 26 November
1943 and 10 February 1944, all of
them in this aircraft. He completed
his tour in the ETO in May 1944
(USAAF)

Fw 190s that were chasing them out of Holland, the American pilots watched on in amazement as the German fighters collided in mid-air.

Two days later 78B Group caught 25 Fw 190s west of Dummer Lake preparing to attack the bombers, and scored eight victories for no losses. This tally included a double for Juchheim and single kills for Turley, who had now claimed six victories in 14 days, and future ace Lt Charles Peal of the 83rd FS.

By the time February ended, the 78th FG had set a new monthly record – 34 victories in 14 missions, for seven losses. 'Big Week' marked the beginning of the end for the Luftwaffe, as most of the German pilots shot down during the offensive had been killed, whilst those that did bail out were often badly wounded. Too many of those lost were experienced pilots who could not be easily replaced by the *Nachwuchs* due to their reduced levels of training.

March 1944 finally saw the daylight offensive reach Berlin, although bad weather prevented the main force from attacking the German capital on the 4th – the first scheduled date for the Berlin mission. B-17s from the 3rd BD and the 4th FG's 336th FS did reach the target, however, after failing to hear the recall.

The weather improved sufficiently on the 6th for Berlin to be attacked in force. The 78th flew escort support, with both groups being sent to the capital. Col Stone led 78A Group to rendezvous with the 1st BD southwest of Dummer Lake, its 36 P-47s providing escort as far as Celle. Here, the group turned back to the west without having made contact, flying along the bomber stream in search of enemy fighters. Five minutes later, 25 Fw 190s hit the 83rd FS as it performed high cover. Combat ranged from 24,000 ft down to 4000 ft over Steinhuder Lake. Two Fw 190s were quickly shot down by Capt Wilkinson and Lt R P Spaulding of the 82nd FS.

Squadronmate Lt Grant Turley then led his flight after three more Focke-Wulfs at low-level, where he got into a turning fight with one, with a second on his tail. Dick Hewitt claimed that he saw Turley score his seventh victory (this was never officially credited to him, however), only for the chasing Fw 190 to close the gap and pull enough deflection to put a burst into the P-47's engine. Turley was unable to bail out before the fighter spun in and exploded near Barenburg.

P-47C-1 41-6345 *Miss Tibbie* of the 82nd FS was the first fighter assigned to future eight-victory ace 2Lt Richard Hewitt. He had joined the unit as a replacement pilot in August 1943 and flew his first combat mission in late September. Hewitt almost certainly claimed his first aerial victory (a Bf 109) in this aircraft on 16 March (*USAAF*)

The Berlin mission on 6 March proved to be the costliest ever mounted by the Eighth Air Force. The Luftwaffe had concentrated its fighters along the route of the bomber stream, sending up an impressive 400 fighters – half of its available force. Both day and nightfighter Bf 110s attacked, as did myriad Bf 109s and Fw 190s. They were opposed by no fewer than 60 P-38s, 100 P-51s and 615 P-47s, whose pilots claimed 81 aircraft destroyed for the loss of 11 fighters. Some 69 B-17s and B-24s of the 672 that reached the target went down, with a further 347 returning with varying degrees of battle damage. When such losses happened on 14 October 1943, they came close to dooming the campaign. Now, the Eighth Air Force had sufficient resources in England to return in strength to Berlin just two days later.

Although the 78th did not claim any aerial success on 8 March, Lt Pete Pompetti and his wingman Lt E S Long strafed an airfield near Bohmte whilst returning from Mannheim. Having hit two Fw 190s, Pompetti then spotted a group of German officers near a staff car and made a quick turn to strafe them. 'They ran into the fields on both sides of the road, and due to my closeness to the ground I do not know whether I hit them or not'.

Quince Brown increased his score on 15 March after he came to the aid of a bomber group that had been bounced by 25 Bf 109s west of Münster. Diving through the only hole in the overcast, Brown caught up with the enemy fighters as they popped out of the overcast and pulled out of their dives at 10,000 ft. Brown and element leader, and future ace, Lt Raymond Smith chased the Bf 109s down to 2000 ft, using their water injection systems to catch up with their opponents. They each sent a fighter down in flames.

Over Strasbourg the next day, Dick Hewitt opened fire from 600 yards with 20 degrees of deflection to hit a Bf 109 that caught fire, rolled inverted and went straight in to explode, giving the future ace his first success. Moments later, Quince Brown got into a fight that element leader 1Lt Ernie Russell later recorded as his most memorable;

'Our time with the bombers had been uneventful – just a lot of tricky crossover turns, rubbernecking, looking for bogeys and being disappointed that the Jerries hadn't turned up. I'm sure the fact that there were no Jerries didn't bother the crews in the "big friends" half as much as it did us.'

After only a few minutes on withdrawal, Brown pulled alongside Russell and pointed down. He and his wingman, 2Lt Ross Orr, followed as Brown and his wingman, 2Lt W N Smith, went looking for 'targets of opportunity'. Brown dove towards Saint Dizier airfield, a major fighter base southeast of Paris. The four P-47s were indicating over 450 mph as Brown shallowed the dive and then pulled out just 100 ft feet above the ground. They were still indicating in excess of 400 mph when Brown hit a Bf 109 in the landing pattern. Russell suddenly found himself 250 yards behind another Messerschmitt approaching to land;

'As the 109 filled my gunsight, I pulled the bright dot in the middle of the glowing ring along his line of flight for a deflection shot of about

30 degrees and squeezed off a burst. Immediately, armour-piercing incendiaries from my guns lit up the grey engine cowling from the prop to the cockpit. My closure rate was so great that I passed over him a fraction of a second later.'

Russell and Orr followed Brown and Smith as the latter pair headed for the southern end of the runway, lining up abreast of each other. 'We made a sharp diving turn and lined up on the runway. We were several hundred feet east of Quince, who was lined up on the runway. A Ju 88 was just about to take off in front of him, while I spotted an Me 110 on a taxiway just to the right of the strip, presenting me with a head-on shot. I centered the needle and ball and waited till he was about 400 yards away, then opened fire. I heard my guns over the roar of my engine at full throttle. Almost instantly, the front of the Me 110 lit up with the flashes of API rounds. I fired until I was less than 200 yards distant, at which point it seemed judicious to pull up.'

Brown destroyed the Ju 88, after which the four P-47 pilots joined up so low that Russell was afraid of hitting the ground as they raced away. 'We had taken the base by surprise, for there was no anti-aircraft fire. However, we strongly suspected we had stirred up a hornets' nest'.

Brown turned northwest as they stayed low until the field was out of sight, before climbing to altitude. Minutes later Russell spotted a mixed group of Bf 109s and Fw 190s diving through the haze. Yelling 'Break Right!', he slammed the throttle into War Emergency Power, turning right as hard as he could to meet the attacker. 'He had the advantage of speed, altitude and position. My lucky break was the fact that he wasn't behind me, and was presented with a tricky firing angle. He missed and flashed past. From experience, I was confident I could out-climb and out-turn him, but more importantly I could "turn on a dime" at the top of a near-vertical climb and "give back change". We called that manoeuvre a "stall turn".

'My chief advantage was that the "Jug" happened to have the fastest aileron roll rate of any fighter, even at low speed. This manoeuvre was fairly simple to perform in a vertical climb at full power. Just before I stalled, I would roll and smoothly apply rudder in the direction I wanted to go, nursing the stick back to get the nose down, and then accelerate. I could almost fly back down the air corridor I had ascended.'

As Russell looked over his shoulder, he saw the Bf 109 doing the same thing;

'I waited for him to be forced into a turn – he committed to a right turn, as I had hoped. I was right at the stall and I rolled left to meet him

Maj Jack Price, CO of the 84th FS, prepares to lead his section aloft from Duxford in P-47D-2 42-74641 *Feather Merchant II* in February 1944. Price had claimed his final two victories in this fighter on 26 November 1943 to 'make ace'. This photograph clearly shows how the 78th could send off two four-aeroplane flights simultaneously on the wide Duxford grass runway. Price's 42-74641 was passed on to fellow ace Lt Peter Pompetti when the former completed his tour at the end of February 1944, but it was downed by flak during a strafing attack on Beauvais airfield on 17 March. Pompetti bailed out and was captured (*USAAF*)

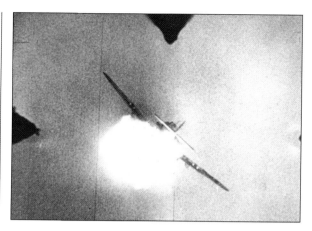

A Bf 109G bursts into flames after being struck by a barrage of 0.50-in shells fired from the eight machine guns of a 78th FG Thunderbolt during a 'Big Week' mission in late February 1944. The group destroyed 12 Bf 109s between 20-25 February (*USAAF*)

head-on. I looked opposite and he was just completing his turn as I pulled out ahead of him. We passed again without firing and I yanked back straight up again. I watched over my shoulder – he was forced to match my climb or run. Up we went. I waited and watched him opposite me, and significantly lower. Finally, he committed to a left turn. I turned in the opposite direction and beat him out.

'Now it was my turn as I manoeuvered into position 45 degrees off his tail. He rolled into a steep left turn, trying to out-turn me, but I was only 150 yards behind him. Like lining up quail, I pulled my sight through him, sensed my lead and pulled the trigger. I gave him a two-second burst that hit his cowling. My next burst dwindled into "pop-pop", as seven of my eight guns jammed! He was less than 50 yards away. To avoid over-running him I pulled up steep and rolled down on him, but he was out of the fight. I now had to worry about the others that were still after us, but my gun camera film later confirmed he was on fire. As I rolled out to meet the next ones, we were suddenly alone in the sky.'

Joining Brown and his wingman Smith, Russell was glad to head home. Moments later, however, the four of them were bounced again. As they broke right, the Germans dove away straight down. Russell recalled, 'Why they decided not to take us on I'll never know. Quince was low on ammunition and I had only one gun working, so I wasn't unhappy to see them go'. Over the Channel, Russell realised that his RAF-issue helmet was soaked wet with sweat.

While he had been engaged in his turning fight with the Messerschmitt, Brown had shot down a second Bf 109 and an Fw 190, thus raising his score to ten (nine aerial and one strafing). He had become the 78th's first 'double ace'. The four pilots from the 84th FS had tangled with II./JG 26 over Saint Dizier, the *Gruppe* recording the loss of three Bf 109s shot down over the field. Additionally, a Ju 88 and a Bf 110 had been destroyed by strafing. VIII Fighter Command eventually confirmed four destroyed for Brown, one destroyed for Russell and one probable for Russell's wingman, Orr. Writing of the mission 50 years later, Russell called it 'the most exciting day of my combat life'. Brown was awarded the Silver Star for his exploits on this day.

On 17 March Lt Peter Pompetti was lost during a strafing mission. Bad weather had split up the three squadrons as they searched for airfield targets over France, with Pompetti and his wingman becoming separated. Spotting a He 111 on Beauvais airfield, the ace bored in on a strafing run, but his Thunderbolt was set alight by flak on his first pass. He pulled straight up and bailed out, successfully evading a search and contacting the local Resistance. That night the group was betrayed by an informant and Pompetti became a PoW.

On 23 March Quince Brown gained his 11th victory following a difficult fight with an Fw 190 he chased through a hole in the clouds over western Germany. His opponent out-manoeuvred him at low altitude over trees when his water injection system failed, but Brown hung on until, in a skid, he nearly rammed the fighter. He opened fire at extremely close range, causing the Fw 190 to explode so violently that Brown had to perform an abrupt wingover at 500 ft to avoid the resulting debris.

The following day Lt J J Hockery downed a Ju 188 to take his growing tally of victories to four.

March 1944 had seen the Luftwaffe hit hard enough that by the end of the month its fighters were no longer rising to oppose USAAF bomber formations as frequently as they once had done. Struggling to find enemy aircraft aloft, the 78th despatched its A and B groups on strafing missions over the Low Countries. Although a solitary Do 217 was downed over Twente airfield, in Holland, by a trio of pilots from the 84th FS (including Quince Brown), strafing accounted for the remaining aircraft destroyed or damaged. A flight from the 82nd FS also sank barges on the Rhine, while another flight destroyed four locomotives east of Wesel, in Germany.

By now, strafing missions were deemed to be just as important as bomber escorts. And the 78th's victory board had a new column for ground targets destroyed, right alongside the one for aerial victories. March ended with the group having flown 21 missions, during which its units claimed twelve aerial and nine strafing victories for the loss of nine pilots in combat and two returning with wounds.

April commenced with yet another strafing mission on the 1st, when Verdun airfield, in France, was attacked. Four days later Ruwer airfield, in Germany, was targeted. Gliders, bombers and transport aircraft were claimed at both sites.

At around this time the 78th FG's Thunderbolts began to appear with their now legendary black-and-white chequerboard cowlings. The reasoning behind the new markings was that with the vast increase in the number of fighter groups in the ETO, individual group formations needed new ways of quick identification to avoid friendly fire incidents. The black chequers were applied after the entire cowling had been painted white, the squares being marked off by tracing the outline of a metal square template. A groundcrewman with a steady hand would then fill in the black area with a brush. All markings were done in this freehand manner, which meant that no two P-47s were painted in exactly the same way.

April also saw the arrival of the first 'silver' P-47s at Duxford. USAAF policy regarding camouflage had changed in November 1943, and directives were issued to manufacturers that it was no longer necessary to paint their products Olive Drab and Neutral Gray. For the groups, this meant that the previous white identification markings and group ID letters were now applied in black onto natural metal aeroplanes.

Bad weather had adversely affected the mission tempo in early April, although on the 8th the 78th managed to strafe two airfields in southwestern Germany. 10 April marked the one-year anniversary of the

The official caption that accompanied this photograph of 1Lt Quince Brown, taken on 17 March 1944, read as follows. 'First man in the European theatre to destroy four German aeroplanes in one day while flying a Republic P-47 Thunderbolt fighter is 1Lt Quince L Brown Jr of Bristow, Oklahoma. For 19 long months a flight instructor at Randolph and Kelly Fields, in Texas, Brown has now shot down ten Jerries since beginning his combat tour in England, five of them in the past two days. On Thursday, 16 March, he destroyed two Messerschmitt 109s and a Focke-Wulf 190 in a terrific air battle, and set a Ju 88 blazing on the ground. The previous day he had "warmed-up" his guns by destroying an ME 109. On Thursday's mission he also damaged two unidentified enemy aeroplanes on the ground. Also to his combat credit are a locomotive and a flak tower. He holds the Air Medal with three Oak Leaf Clusters and the DFC with one cluster' (*USAAF*)

1Lt James Wilkinson inspects cannon damage to his P-47D with his crew chief in a Duxford hangar. This photograph was taken in late February/early March 1944, as the Thunderbolt has only three victory markings beneath its cockpit. Wilkinson scored his fourth kill on 6 March 1944 (*USAAF*)

first mission flown by the group over Europe. It proved to be a memorable occasion for 83rd FS pilots 1Lts Juchheim and Peal, who between them destroyed no fewer than eight enemy aircraft during strafing runs on an airfield near Romorantin, in France. Pilots from the unit were credited with no fewer than 13 aircraft destroyed. Juchheim downed an Fw 190 over Lüneburg, Germany, the following day.

On 12 April the group flew what its pilots felt was 'the most fouled-up' mission ever assigned to them, with the bombers finally aborting over Aachen due to cloud cover and dense contrails. Despite the poor atmospheric conditions, combat did happen during 78A Group's return flight home. Quince Brown was at the head of the group near Duren when 30 Fw 190s and Bf 109s emerged from the clouds below them, heading in the opposite direction. Brown immediately led the 84th FS down after them, the German pilots breaking formation as they dove for the deck. Brown hit an Fw 190 in its drop tank, which exploded – he flew through the flame and debris.

Shortly thereafter, a flight of 82nd FS machines, led by Capt John Hockery, spotted a German aircraft diving through clouds near Sedan, in France. Having followed the lone aircraft, they soon found six Ju 87 Stukas milling around above Ensheim airfield, in Germany, with another 50 dive-bombers on the ground. The four American pilots each bagged a Stuka, before setting several more on fire during a devastating strafing run. Capt Hockery's Ju 87 kill made him an aerial ace – Lt Juchheim achieved this accolade with an Fw 190 destroyed over Büchenbeuren, Germany, the following day.

The strafing successes by the 78th, 4th and 20th FGs in particular during early April led VIII Fighter Command to mount dedicated multi-group strafing missions to central Germany on several occasions during the latter half of April. The 78th participated in the operation on the 15th and lost three pilots and their P-47s to bad weather without a single enemy aircraft being fired upon.

On 30 April, Alwin Juchheim was again amongst the victories when he engaged two Fw 190s over Dreux, in France. The pilot of the first fighter he targeted bailed out successfully, while his second opponent tried to escape at low-level. He met with a fiery demise, however, when the German clipped the ground with his propellor, the Fw 190 digging a wingtip in and exploding on impact. With this success, and two other Fw 190s downed by his squadronmates, the 78th FG's total was 17 aerial and 29 strafing kills, as well as 28 locomotives destroyed during 22 missions. Seven pilots had been lost to all causes.

April also saw eight pilots from the group successfully complete their 200-hour combat tours. While VIII Fighter Command tried to urge such individuals to extend their tours by a further 50 hours, most did not take up the offer. In May, the combat tour for fighter pilots was extended to 250 hours, causing much grumbling in the ranks. Even with this increase,

during May and June 1944 the 78th would be transformed by the departure of nearly half of its tour-expired combat veterans and their replacement by newly trained pilots from the USA. Additionally, P-47 squadrons were reduced in size to 28 aircraft so that additional Thunderbolts could be transferred to Ninth Air Force groups in preparation for the D-Day invasion.

On 1 May operational control of the Eighth Air Force and RAF Bomber Command shifted to Gen Dwight D Eisenhower's Supreme Headquarters of the Allied Expeditionary Forces (SHAEF). In the lead up to D-Day, heavy bombers and their escorts would now be sent against tactical targets in northwestern France and the Low Countries, rather than strategic targets in Germany.

Bad weather during the first week of May resulted in both heavy bombers and Thunderbolt groups being sent on missions against 'Noball' V1 sites in northern France, whose flak defences were on par with those found protecting industrial targets in Germany – a clear indication of their importance.

The first real action for the 78th in May came on the 11th when the 82nd FS strafed Dijon airfield, in France, destroying three aircraft. Three Fw 190s were also shot down by the 83rd and 84th FSs near Orleans and Montargis that same day.

P-47D-6 42-74742 *"WAR EAGLE"* has its engine run up at Duxford in the spring of 1944 following a spell of routine maintenance. Note the fighter's newly applied black/white chequerboard marking on the cowling, which was adopted by the 78th as its group identifier from April 1944. This aircraft enjoyed a long career with the 84th FS, initially being assigned to 1Lt Julius Maxwell (who subsequently shot down the 300th German aeroplane credited to the 78th FG on 31 December 1944). Having flown 90 missions, 42-74742 was damaged beyond repair in a landing accident at Duxford on 15 December 1944 whilst being flown by Lt Earl Stier (*USAAF*)

Groundcrew prepare to attach newly painted chequerboard cowling panels to a recently arrived P-47D of the 83rd FS in April 1944. Unpainted Thunderbolts first began to reach groups in the ETO in late March 1944 following the USAAF's decision to discontinue factory camouflage paint in November 1943. Note the visiting P-47D from the 353rd FG parked in the background (*USAAF*)

An Fw 190 disintegrates as its drop tank explodes under fire from Capt William May of the 82nd FS during a low altitude combat near Dummer Lake on 9 April 1944. May served with the 78th FG from February 1943 through to VE Day, moving from the 82nd FS to the group HQ after he completed his tour. This Fw 190 proved to be May's final aerial success (*USAAF*)

May also saw the Eighth Air Force join the Fifteenth Air Force in targeting Germany's oil industry, although this campaign was not officially recognised by SHAEF since its priority was invasion targets. Indeed, the Fifteenth Air Force had begun targeting German oil production facilities in April with renewed attacks on the huge refinery at Ploesti, in Rumania, from its bases in Italy. The first Eighth Air Force mission against Germany's synthetic oil industry (which provided the Wehrmacht with two-thirds of its fuel requirements) came on 12 May. No fewer than 814 bombers targeted the synthetic oil factories at Zwickau, in Germany, and Brux, in Czechoslovakia. The Luftwaffe, which had been reluctant to oppose recent missions, sent up more than 200 interceptors in defence of these vital plants.

Twenty-five miles west of Koblenz, Group 78A spotted 100 Fw 190s closing on the lead bombers. Two flights from the 82nd FS turned into them and deflected many of the attackers, while the other two flights chased enemy fighters as they dove away. Mission leader Capt James Wilkinson hit an Fw 190 from 200 yards astern and it caught fire and hit the ground without the pilot bailing out. This was Wilkinson's fifth aerial success. On the deck, Lt Robert Baker struck his Fw 190 in its engine from 400 yards and the German pilot bailed out, hitting the ground before his parachute could deploy. Former bomber pilot Lt Daniel Hagarty set an Fw 190 on fire as it started to dive away, then caught a second fighter at deck level, where he hit it in the wingroot gun bay with the last of his ammunition. The explosion blew the Focke-Wulf's wing off, after which it snap-rolled end over end into the trees and exploded. Having been separated from his squadronmates during the engagement, and no longer able to defend himself, Hagarty was forced to bail out over Trier minutes later after his P-47 was shot up by yet more Fw 190s.

Back at altitude, Lt Merle Capp hit an Fw 190 as it opened fire on the bombers. The Luftwaffe pilot released his canopy, which hit Capp's wing as the pilot bailed out. Ben Watkins forced an Fw 190 to break off when he

Recently promoted Capt Quince Brown was issued with brand new P-47D-21 42-25698 in early May 1944, although he failed to make any claims in it. The official caption that accompanied this photograph, which was released for publication by the War Department on 20 May 1944, read as follows. 'Preparatory to starting the engine of the P-47 Thunderbolt piloted by Capt Quince Brown, leading fighter pilot with 13 kills to his credit, crew chief TSgt Bill C Jensen of Superior, Nebraska, and assistant crew chief Cpl Thomas W Stoker of Oklahoma City, Oklahoma, pull through the prop by hand in order to clear oil from the cylinders'. This aircraft was downed by flak near Grafenhausen on 10 September 1944, Lt Robert Clague making a forced landing southwest of Darmstadt and becoming a PoW (*USAAF*)

was spotted by his opponent, chasing the fighter down to 10,000 ft, where he hit it. Watkins later reported that 'the Kraut sailed out and hit my left wing, and I returned with part of his 'chute caught on my left wingtip'.

At the mission briefing on 19 May, Col Stone announced that the 78th FG had scored 198 aerial victories to date. Later that day the group would add 12 kills to its tally during a highly successful escort for B-24s over Dummer Lake, the bombers targeting Brunswick's aircraft factories. As the 'heavies' approached the target, a formation of 60 Fw 190s made a '12 o'clock high' 'Company Front' attack against the lead bombers. As Capt James Wilkinson recalled, 'We got behind the first wave of 30 and broke them up, then turned into the second wave. I hit one at 200 yards and he bailed out'.

At much the same time, on the other side of the formation, Lt Merle Capp spotted Bf 109s coming in and turned his flight to break them up. He closed behind the leader and hit him so hard with a long burst of fire that the fighter exploded in midair. Spotting 40 more Fw 190s closing on the B-24s, Lt Myron Woller and his flight succeeded in breaking up this attack, after which Woller chased a fighter to the deck and watched as one of its wheels dropped down following his first burst of fire. The extended undercarriage leg struck the ground when Woller fired again, causing the Fw 190 to cartwheel and explode.

Separated from his flight, Lt Herbert Boyle of the 84th FS saw an Fw 190 in a spin and gave chase. Moments later the German pilot pulled out, only to find a P-47 on his tail. After three bursts, the fighter's propellor was windmilling, and Boyle pulled up alongside his quarry to see the pilot dead in the cockpit. After Boyle had returned to Duxford his crew chief found both oil and blood on the cowling of his fighter.

Over Steinhuder Lake, 78B Group spotted more German fighters. Capt William Hunt, flying element lead for Col Stone, saw two P-47s from another group burst into flames as they attacked the enemy aircraft, then spotted the Bf 109 that had shot them down. Giving chase in a vertical dive, Hunt saw pieces start to fly off the fighter after he opened fire. The Bf 109 went out of control at 6000 ft and exploded when it hit the ground at high speed.

Future ace 2Lt Merle Capp of the 82nd FS poses for the camera shortly after claiming his first aerial success (an Fw 190) on 12 May 1944 over Koblenz. He would down a Bf 109 near Dummer Lake exactly one week later, this victory earning him a prize. On 18 May group leader Col Stone had announced that the 78th FG's tally of aerial victories had reached 198, and that a loving cup would be awarded to the pilot who scored number 200. During the next day's escort to Brunswick, Merle Capp exploded a Bf 109G with a long burst to claim the group's 200th victory (*USAAF via John M Dibbs/Plane Picture Company*)

Lt Harold Beck of the 82nd FS had the closest call of all on 19 May, when his P-47 was hit in its supercharger. With his fighter now significantly down on power, Beck struggled to fend off four Bf 109s that took it in turns to shoot at him. Oil covered the windscreen, the fighter's hydraulic pressure dropped and its gyro compass and airspeed indicator were shot out. With RPM down to 2500 and oil pressure at just ten pounds, the P-47's oil temperature went to maximum. Beck was sure the engine would explode.

With three Bf 109s still behind him, he dove vertically to 2000 ft, which put out a fire that had started in the engine. At this point two of the enemy fighters left, apparently out of ammunition. Beck then briefly lost sight of the third, the fighter reappearing in close formation off his right wingtip! After a few moments the German pilot saluted his opponent and then split-essed for home, also out of ammunition. Beck flew home using his magnetic compass, fighting to control the P-47 as its trim tabs had also been shot out.

Flying over the Dutch coast, the aircraft's oil pressure dropped to zero and cylinder head temperature went to maximum. Beck immediately dove from 12,000 ft down to 4000 ft in solid haze without instruments in an attempt to cool the engine. As he crossed the English coast, the engine froze up completely. Spotting an airfield below him, Beck shook his wheels down, dead-stick landed on the runway and rolled to a stop without brakes. Ground personnel counted ten 20 mm shell hits in the fuselage in addition to numerous small-calibre holes throughout the airframe. The propellor had also been holed and the tops shot off two engine cylinders. The P-47 could definitely 'take it'.

On 22 May the 78th had a stand-down day, with a party held in the Officer's Club for Col Stone, who had completed his tour and was replaced by Col Frederick C Gray Jr. Aged 33, the latter was an 'old' Regular Army officer who would subsequently become the group's most-loved leader since the late Col Peterson.

Two days later Gray led the group's first 'Droopsnoot' bombing mission. Guided by a modified P-38J (flown by 84th FS CO Maj Harold Stump) that housed a bombardier and a Norden bombsight in its nose, the 78th hit a railway bridge over the River Oise, south of Creil, in France. Bombing when signalled from 18,000 ft, the group destroyed half of the bridge.

French airfields were strafed the following day, while Capt Alwin Juchheim and Lt W M McDermott of the 83rd FS also shot down a Bf 109 each near Saint-Dizier. Juchheim claimed his ninth, and last, aerial success on 27 May when he was credited with a Bf 109 over Freiburg, in Germany. This was the group's only claim that day.

Bad weather over central and eastern Germany, coupled with good weather over French invasion targets meant that the next strike against the synthetic oil industry did not happen until 28 May, when a record 1341 B-17s and B-24s sortied against various targets. The Luftwaffe opposed the raids with 300 fighters.

This mission saw the end of Capt Alwin Juchheim's fighter career when a P-51B from the 363rd FG collided with him head-on, shearing a wing off the P-47 and sending it spinning earthwards. Although the Mustang pilot was killed instantly, Juchheim managed to break free from the spinning debris and bail out. A Bf 109 then attempted to strafe him in his parachute, but fellow flight members Lts William McDermott and Fred White covered his descent. White hit the German machine, which sprayed the American's windscreen with glycol. McDermott then closed in and despatched the damaged fighter just as Juchheim landed safely and was captured. Two pilots from the 82nd FS were not so lucky that day, however, both men being killed by German flak.

May ended with Maj Stump leading another 'Droopsnoot' mission, the group dropping 50 500-lb bombs on the railway bridge at Beaumont-sur-Oise, in France, destroying its abutments at both ends.

The 78th had completed 25 missions in May, suffering eight losses and claiming 25 aerial victories, four strafing victories and 20 locomotives destroyed. Amongst the leading 'loco strafers' in the group was acting 82nd FS CO, and ace, Capt James Wilkinson, who believed that if an engine was hit in the right places it could be put out of action for months rather than weeks. The RAF was keen for him to demonstrate his theory, and arranged for a real locomotive to serve as a target in Wales. The exercise was scheduled for 4 June, but bad weather en route from Duxford held up Wilkinson's flight clearance. In an effort to get airborne he radioed the control tower and stated that he was going on a local test flight. Heading west for Wales, Wilkinson flew into a mist-shrouded mountain near Llandovery, in Carmarthenshire, south Wales, and was killed.

Thanks to the efforts of men like Capt James Wilkinson, the Battle of Germany had now been won, as the Luftwaffe was a spent force in comparison to what it had been on New Year's Day 1944. The airmen of the USAAF had set the stage for the opening of the Second Front.

Capt Alwin Juchheim of the 83rd FS claimed nine aerial and six strafing victories prior to suffering a midair collision with a P-51B from the 363rd FG during an aerial battle near Gardelegen, Germany, on 28 May 1944. Juchheim managed to extricate himself from the spinning P-47, but the Mustang pilot perished. When a Bf 109 attempted to strafe Juchheim in his parachute, fellow flight members Lts William McDermott and Fred White covered his descent. White hit the German machine, which sprayed the American's windscreen with glycol. McDermott then closed in and despatched the damaged fighter just as Juchheim landed safely and was captured (*USAAF*)

LIBERATING EUROPE

6 June 1944 really was the longest day. Double-Daylight Saving Time meant dawn came around at 0300 hrs. The night sky had been filled for hours with the drone of aircraft – bombers heading toward invasion targets and transports carrying British and American paratroops. As groundcrewman Warren Kellerstadt recalled;

'They didn't tell us when D-Day was going to be, but the night before we could smell something in the wind. They closed up the base tight and wouldn't let anyone on or off, and right after supper on 5 June VIII Fighter Command HQ ordered that black and white stripes be painted around the wings and fuselages of our aeroplanes. We armourers were kept busy all night lugging bombs from the dump out to the dispersal area to stack next to the aeroplanes. I worked until midnight, then had guard duty from 0200 hrs. All night long the bombers went out, first the RAF, then ours. They all had their navigation lights on because there were so many of them, and the sky looked like a Christmas tree, full of red and green lights.'

Along with the other P-47 groups of both the Eighth and Ninth Air Forces, the main work of the 78th FG in the immediate wake of the invasion was dive-bombing. According to Kellerstadt, 'All day long they flew back and forth, dive-bombing and strafing everything that moved in Normandy. When they returned from a mission we hopped on the aeroplanes, rearmed and bombed them, and cleaned as many of the guns as we had time for before they took off again'. With losses significantly up following D-Day, groundcrews were kept busy preparing replacement aircraft when not working on P-47s already in group service.

The first D-Day mission for the 78th saw pilots crank their engines into life at 0320 hrs on 6 June. Rain was pouring down and visibility was so bad that pilot Lt Richard Holly remembered that when Col Gray's first section took off, 'He just barely cleared the end of the runway before he was out of sight'. Holly instructed his flight to set their gyros on his and follow him. 'It was the only instrument takeoff I made in the war, and it was also the only one I made with water injection all the way because we were so heavily laden with ordnance and fuel'.

Nearly every pilot who flew on D-Day recalled that the biggest problem they faced was avoiding mid-air collisions with aeroplanes from other units, as there were so many Allied aircraft airborne. The pilots of the 78th found themselves flying in and out of rain showers as they crossed the Channel. While passing through a rainstorm, they encountered a formation of Lancasters and barely avoided disaster. Once they neared France, Holly remembered, 'I did not see anything on the ground through the clouds, but the red glow below the clouds told us it was Omaha Beach. With the approach of daylight the red glow went away, but we knew from the smoke and haze that there was still plenty going on down there'.

The 78th flew three missions on D-Day. With both A and B groups operating, aeroplanes were landing and taking off at Duxford all day long. Eight-aircraft fighter-bombing attacks were made on targets inland, with

P-47D-22 42-25871 *NIGGER II!* of Capt Richard Holly, acting CO of the 84th FS, had originally been delivered to the unit in natural metal finish in mid June 1944. On 25 June it was hit by flak, which left 32 shrapnel holes in the wings and fuselage. Hastily repaired, the fighter was hit in the left wing by flak four days later. The damaged flying surface was replaced with an olive drab/ neutral grey camouflaged wing, and two weeks later the rest of the aeroplane was painted in RAF Dark Green (note the lighter colour of the left wing and unpainted canopy frame and cockpit interior), with RAF Sky undersurfaces. The fighter's unfortunate nickname refers to Capt Holly's wife, who was a dedicated sunbather (*USAAF via John M Dibbs/Plane Picture Company*)

the 83rd FS targeting a railway bridge 40 miles west of Paris, while the 84th FS hit the Alençon railway marshalling yard and blew up a nearby ammunition dump.

On the second mission of the day the 83rd FS, led by Col Gray, engaged in aerial combat. As the unit approached Mayenne railway marshalling yard, eight Fw 190s were spotted on the deck. Two flights went after the German fighters, Lt Peter Caulfield singling one out and performing a 'Lufbery Circle' in order to get onto its tail. Pulling 90 degrees deflection and firing, he saw the Fw 190 snap-roll, spin, pull out, turn and hit the ground with a wingtip, causing it to crash and explode. Col Gray and his wingman Lt Vincent Massa pursued several Fw 190s, catching up with them thanks to water-injection. Gray began firing at the 'tail-end Charlie', watching his canopy come off and the engine quit. He then overshot his opponent, leaving Massa to pull in behind the fighter and give it the *coup de grace*.

The final mission of the 'Longest Day' commenced at 1800 hrs when 32 aircraft were sent to patrol between Chaillone and La Coulonche. Two flights from the 84th FS strafed a locomotive pulling fuel tanks, and it exploded so violently that debris hit the attacking P-47s. Lt Wallace Hailey had to abandon his machine over the Channel, where he was rescued by ASR, while two other damaged Thunderbolts managed to land safely at Ford.

The following day the 84th FS engaged Bf 109s near Montdidier, and four enemy fighters were downed. Future aces Capt Benjamin Mayo and Lt Dorian Ledington both claimed their first victories during this action.

10 June saw the 78th suffer its worst ever day in combat, with no fewer than ten P-47s being shot down. Seven pilots were killed, one was captured and two evaded. During the first attack of the day, near Le Touquet, in France, one P-47 was hit by flak and downed and a second hit trees while strafing targets of opportunity. A third fighter from this mission crash-landed near Duxford upon its return to base.

Original group member, and 84th FS CO, Maj Harold Stump led 40 P-47s of the 83rd and 84th FSs aloft at 1245 hrs on the first mission of his second tour – a dive-bombing attack southwest of Argentan. As Stump and the rest of the first flight pulled up from dropping their bombs, 20 Bf 109s that were reportedly wearing D-Day stripes and fake British insignia engaged the diving P-47. Although most of the Thunderbolt pilots

Col Fred Gray replaced Col Stone as group CO on 22 May 1944, and the former is seen here standing in front of his P-47D-25 42-26391 *"Mr. Ted"* with unidentified groundcrew on 10 July 1944. Gray proved to be the 78th's most popular group commander after its original CO, Arman Peterson, as he always chose to fly the tough missions. 42-26391 was the second Thunderbolt assigned to Gray, his first aircraft being P-47D-22 42-25996. He later flew P-51D-20 44-63279, which, like his Thunderbolts, was maintained by the 83rd FS (*USAAF*)

quickly jettisoned their bombs and turned into the attacking enemy machines, Majs Stump and William Hunt and 2Lt Daniel Loyd of the lead flight perished when they were shot down during that first pass.

The airspace beneath the low cloud deck and the ground was immediately filled by a maelstrom of wildly manoeuvring aircraft. Dorian Ledington salvoed his bombs as a Bf 109 flew past him, and he fired into its wing root – the pilot bailed out. As Lt Luther Abel pulled off the target after dropping his bombs, he spotted an enemy fighter that appeared to be out of range of his guns. Firing at it nevertheless, Abel was astonished to see the Bf 109 burst into flames and the pilot bail out. His squadronmate Lt Robert McIntosh destroyed an Fw 190 that had joined the fight, but he was in turn brought down by another one moments later, bailing out and becoming an evader.

Lt Franklin Pursell of the 83rd FS found 15 Fw 190s and got one, while squadronmate Capt Robert Ealey out-climbed a Bf 109 and shot it down. A second Messerschmitt that was pursuing Ealey was destroyed by squadronmate Maj Donald McLeod, who was then hit by a third fighter and forced to bail out. Lucky to meet up with the Resistance, McLeod walked the ground below the battle of 10 June three days later and discovered the body of his friend Lt Vincent Massa, who had also been shot down and killed during the fight.

Fortunately for the 78th FG, these losses were quickly made good by the return of pilots like Capt Dick Hewitt of the 82nd FS who had completed their first tours and subsequently volunteered for a second following their mandatory 30-day leave back home. The death of Maj Stump, killed on his first mission of his second tour, became a matter of concern to many of the 'retreads' over the summer, however, with several who had survived 200-hour tours in late 1943 and the first half of 1944 going missing in their first few missions after their return to the 78th. This was a reflection of the very different kind of combat they were now engaged in. Outflying an enemy with piloting skill had little to do with whether one survived at low level, where flak – both German and 'friendly' – was a constant concern over the battlefield.

63

The rest of June and most of July saw the 78th heavily involved in air support for the Battle of Normandy, with multiple missions being flown nearly every day in often marginal weather. Despite the focus being on strafing and fighter-bomber missions, seven Bf 109s and Fw 190s were downed by the group through to 30 June – Capt Mayo got his second kill on the 20th, for example. The last success of the month was a strafing victory on 30 June credited to future 82nd FS ace Lt Herbert Shope.

As losses mounted and new pilots joined the group, some proved to be rather different to the veterans they replaced. Crew Chief James Tudor recalled;

'Some young pilots coming into the unit gave us mechanics a fit. While flying your aeroplane on a mission, they would get as far as the Channel when all of a sudden the engine would begin to act up, so back to base they came. The write-up in the Form One was familiar – "Engine runs excessively rough", or "Prop surges at a given altitude". Some of these guys we hated to draw once we got to know them because you could predict an abort with a high degree of accuracy. Some overcame it after a few trips, others never did.'

Among the new pilots was 2Lt Frank Oiler, assigned to the 82nd FS. As he recalled many years after the war, even with operations at such a high tempo in the summer of 1944, the squadron did its best to give a new pilot as much time to learn what he needed to survive as it could. During his first two weeks with the unit, he flew only local flights, getting used to the English weather, which was a far cry from what he had experienced in the USA. By the end of that time, he had doubled the number of instrument flight hours in his logbook and felt comfortable taking off from Duxford, only to disappear into a cloud within a minute – he would stick with his leader until they 'broke out on top'.

Operational missions began shortly thereafter, with new pilots like Oiler taking whatever aeroplane was available at the time. After three successful missions, he was fortunate enough to be assigned an older P-47D 'razorback' as his own aircraft when its regular pilot received one of the new 'bubbletop' Thunderbolts issued to the 78th from June 1944. Oiler's aeroplane would be memorable due to his choice of personal insignia – a large colourful wasp complete with a prominent stinger, and the name *Eileen*. He would have this artwork reapplied to a new P-47D-25 in late August when the first *Eileen* went the way of all war-weary Thunderbolts and was turned into a source of spare parts.

1Lt Frank Oiler's P-47D-28 42-28878 *Eileen* had the most spectacular artwork of any 78th FG Thunderbolt, the fighter being named after the pilot's girlfriend. Assigned to the group in September 1944, it remained with the 84th FS until the unit switched to the Mustang at the end of the year. 42-28878 was then sent to the 56th FG as an attrition replacement (*USAAF*)

The 78th FG routinely performed eight-aircraft takeoffs in close formation, allowing two flights to depart side-by-side. If pilots were not careful in maintaining direction, however, collisions like this one on 1 July 1944 were inevitable, though fortunately rare. 83rd FS pilots Lts Edward Kitley and Cleon Raese both perished in this accident, their heavily loaded P-47s colliding shortly after taking off from Duxford in a high crosswind (*USAAF*)

Acting 84th FS CO Capt Richard Holly was the recipient of a new silver Thunderbolt in late June. Returning home in bad weather from his first mission in the aircraft, the flight was hit by radar-directed flak;

'Although I couldn't get away from the flak, fortunately, none of it had penetrated into the cockpit and there didn't seem to be anything wrong with my ship. Nevertheless, they had me so zeroed that I was seriously considering bailing out. Sticking with my P-47, I finally got out of the flak and looked around. I could see flak holes all over my wings, but the aircraft didn't seem to have suffered any structural damage.'

Holly rejoined the rest of his flight, only to run into another heavy flak concentration a short while later that inflicted damage on three of the four P-47s. 'Evidently, we'd flown over the "postgraduates" of all flak gunners. When I got the aeroplane home, my crew counted 32 holes. Each hole required a patch, and it seemed a shame that a brand new aeroplane like that ended up covered in patches.'

Holly's crew chief, Sgt 'Dusty' Bauer, had the Thunderbolt ready to fly again in two days. Holly then flew it on a low-level mission. 'We were shooting up trains and flak towers, and I took a cannon shell smack in the leading edge of the left wing, jamming two of the guns'. Holly brought the P-47 home again, and this time the crew found that its main spar had been broken as a result of the flak hit – the left wing needed to be replaced. Bauer could not find another unpainted wing, so a camouflaged one was used instead. The rest of the aeroplane remained in natural metal. 'I flew it like that for the next two or three weeks', Holly recalled. 'Eventually I decided it was kind of showing off a little too much, so we painted the rest of it to match the new wing and I lost my pretty silver aeroplane. "Dusty" Bauer was a great crew chief, and he kept that aeroplane flying no matter what happened'.

This kind of low-level air combat cemented in pilots' minds how lucky they were to be flying the virtually indestructible Thunderbolt.

By the end of June the group had flown 45 missions and claimed 20 aerial victories, one strafing victory and 13 locomotives destroyed. In return, 13 pilots had been killed, two captured and two evaded – the heaviest monthly loss the group had yet experienced. The 83rd FS had been the high-time unit that month, flying 639 sorties –14 pilots had aborted and eight failed to take off successfully. The squadron had fired 78,000 rounds and dropped 78.9 tons of bombs, with pilots averaging 78 flying hours each – a new group record.

June had been rough and July would be almost as bad, with the 78th continuing to support the Allied breakout in the Norman bocage. The first week of July saw aerial combat take place on at least one mission per day as the Luftwaffe funnelled more *Jagdgeschwadern* from Germany into Normandy. On 1 July, the 78A Group mission was hit by Bf 109s and Fw 190s as the fighters crossed the frontlines, Lt Ross Orr of the 84th FS being killed. He was the third pilot to perish that day, for at the very start of this mission two heavily loaded P-47s had collided shortly after taking off from Duxford in a bad crosswind.

Quickly turning into the German fighters as they dived on them at 12,000 ft over St Quentin, the P-47 pilots managed to claim three enemy aircraft destroyed. It had been Lt James Stallings of the 82nd FS that had spotted the German fighters diving on the Thunderbolts, whose pilots jettisoned their bombs at his warning. Stallings was only able to avoid the fighters by throwing his P-47 into a violent spin. Recovering at 3000 ft, he discovered he had no elevator trim. 'In fact, I'd taken two 20 mm cannon shells in my tail, and was darn lucky my controls weren't completely gone', he remembered. 'I had to keep a lot of forward pressure on the stick to fly straight and level'.

The danger of 'friendly fire' was also ever present during this period. On 5 July Lt William Newton of the 84th FS was killed when his P-47 was shot down by a Spitfire near Breteuil, in France. Four days later Lt Jack Miller of the 83rd FS was returning to England, having had to abort due to failing oil pressure, when his P-47 was shot up by several Spitfires over the Bay of Seine. His Thunderbolt had been mistaken for an Fw 190, despite its prominent D-Day stripes. Miller bailed out and was picked up by an Allied beach patrol. Taken to a beachhead airfield, he was flown back to Duxford in an Anson.

On a more positive note, future ace Maj William Julian of the 83rd FS had claimed his third kill on 5 July and the group had downed five Fw 190s the following day – one of these had provided future 84th FS ace Lt Charles Parmelee with his first success.

On 25 June 1944, the 78th FG's acting group ops officer Maj Robert Eby suffered serious flak damage to the flaps of his P-47D-25 during a strafing mission over the Normandy battlefield. His first instinct was to bail out, but his wingman spotted a British landing ground near the beachhead and guided him to it. Eby landed 'hot' without flaps on the short strip, using every inch of it to come to a successful stop (*USAAF*)

Col Fred Gray (standing seventh from the left) joins Maj Ben Mayo (standing eighth from the left) and his pilots from the 82nd FS during a squadron photograph at Duxford on 5 July 1944 (*USAAF*)

Maj Ben Mayo, CO of the 82nd FS, poses for the base photographer on the wing root of his P-47D-25 42-26671 *No Guts – No Glory!* shortly after claiming his second aerial victory on 20 June 1944. Mayo had been transferred in from the 84th FS (with whom he had claimed an aerial victory on 7 June 1944) to become CO of the 82nd FS on 8 June 1944 following the death of the unit's acting commanding officer, Capt James Wilkinson, in a flying accident on 4 June. Mayo returned to the 84th FS as its new CO on 13 July (replacing the tour-expired Capt Richard Holly), and ended his tour with a score of four aerial and 2.5 strafing victories. 42-26671 remained with the 82nd following the departure of Mayo, who subsequently flew 42-26567 with the 84th (*USAAF via John M Dibbs/Plane Picture Company*)

Having failed to claim any enemy aircraft destroyed for almost two weeks, the 78th endured a day of mixed fortunes on 19 July. That morning, 84th FS CO Maj Ben Mayo led 78A Group on the first deep-penetration escort mission flown by the unit since the invasion. As the P-47 pilots weaved over the lead bombers, an airfield crowded with aeroplanes was spotted at Eutingen, in Germany. Ten minutes later, when the 84th FS's relief arrived, the Thunderbolts broke away from the bombers and went back to hit the airfield. Dropping low some 20 miles out, as per standard doctrine, they made a sweeping pass over the base, which was only lightly protected by flak. Mayo saw that the first strafing run had been successful, and called for a second run, which was even more productive. Five pilots from the 84th blew up seven Ju 188s, Do 217s, Ju 87s and Me 410s.

The 83rd FS, meanwhile, had found more Ju 188s at an airfield near Koblenz. Seven were destroyed, along with a lone Do 217 – the latter was the first victory credited to future ace Capt Robert Bonebrake.

As the squadron pulled away from the burning airfield, 82nd FS CO Maj Doug Munson, flying his fourth mission of his second tour, spotted another airfield at Freudenstadt, west of Stuttgart. Leading his squadron in an attack against Ju 52/3ms, he destroyed two and shared a third with Lt Jim Kinsolving. Again, the defences were light, and Munson called for a second run. As Kinsolving remembered, 'He got good hits on a second Ju 52/3m, but then he appeared to take a flak hit and nosed down. His P-47 struck the ground at a slight angle and burst into flame'. Munson had been a popular commander, and his loss was hard to take. But worse was to come in the afternoon.

A pilot with the 401st BG who was a close friend of Lts John Putnam and Martin Smith of the 84th FS flew his B-17 to Duxford for a visit at around 1330 hrs. His friends climbed aboard and the bomber pilot proceeded to perform a 'beat-up' of Duxford airfield. Turning for a second run, he descended to a height of less than 50 ft across the grass runway and headed straight for a line of hangars. Pulling up too late to clear the 84th's hangar, he struck a beacon atop the structure. The left wing outboard of the engines was torn off, taking half the left stabiliser with it as it bent back. The bomber rolled onto its back, dropping part of the wing on the roof of the Officer's Club and then roared over the baseball field, with the players taking off in all directions. It then hit the roof of the barracks housing the enlisted men of the 83rd FS.

Full of fuel, the bomber exploded, destroying a major section of the two-storey brick building and killing Sgt Ernest Taylor. Two other men escaped with serious burns. The 13 personnel aboard the bomber all perished. Chaplain William Zink became the first Eighth Air Force Chaplain to be awarded the Soldier's Medal for his heroism in rescuing the victims in the barracks. Shortly thereafter, Lt Gen Doolittle made low-level buzzing a court-martial offence in the Eighth Air Force.

Remarkable differences in the camouflage and markings worn by the P-47s at Duxford became more apparent from July onwards. Since late April, all new replacement aircraft had arrived unpainted in natural aluminium. Following the low-level combat over Normandy in the wake of the invasion, most pilots flying fighter-bomber missions felt that 'silver' aeroplanes left them open to being spotted too easily by the many German fighters that had bounced the group from above, often with devastating results.

First to go, by order of SHAEF, in mid-July were the black-and-white 'invasion stripes' on the uppersurfaces of the wings and fuselage. At the same time this was done, aircraft were repainted in a more complete camouflage as per an order issued by VIII Fighter Command. The group maintenance unit was able to locate stocks of RAF paint, and from late July all 'silver' P-47s were fully camouflaged with RAF Dark Green uppersurfaces and RAF Sky undersides. Black and white D-Day stripes were reapplied on the undersides of the wings and fuselage due to the many incidents of 'friendly fire' experienced when flying over Allied ground units in France.

On 25 July the 78th put up a maximum effort mission to Saint-Lô, in Normandy. Following the bombing of the German frontlines by more than 700 B-17s and B-24s, the 78th joined P-47s from the 56th and 353rd FGs in bombing and strafing the recently attacked German positions near the battered city. With the breakout from Saint-Lô, the battle for Normandy came to an end and the liberation of the rest of France began.

By month-end the 78th FG had flown 28 missions and shot down nine aircraft, with a further 20 destroyed during strafing attacks. Some 21 locomotives had also been wrecked and every other kind of transportation target hit. These successes had cost the group seven pilots killed in action, three as PoWs and one recovered. Two pilots had also perished in the B-17 accident.

Ground attack missions continued to take a toll in August, with the 82nd FS losing a second commanding officer within two weeks on 2 August when Capt Charles Clark went down to become a PoW. He was replaced by group newcomer Maj Joseph Myers, who already had three victories from his time with the 55th FG – he would go on to make ace with his new unit.

10 August saw all three squadrons within the 78th claim a large number of strafing victories, the action starting when the 83rd FS, led by Capt Charles Peal, spotted 30 He 111s and Ju 52/3ms parked under camouflage netting at Château-Salins airfield, in France. Ten pilots, including future 83rd FS aces Capt Charles Peal, Lt Robert Green, Capt Robert Bonebrake

Maj Ben Mayo had received brand new P-47D-25 42-26551 in late May 1944, and had shot down a Bf 109 over Montdidier with it on 7 June. He was transferred to the 82nd FS as its CO the following day, leaving this aircraft behind (*USAAF*)

The impressive scoreboard of the 82nd FS at Duxford on 26 July 1944. By VE Day the squadron had been credited with 102.5 aerial victories, ten probables and 39.5 damaged and 94.5 strafing victories and 117 damaged. The 82nd also ended the war as the group's top 'train-busting' squadron (*USAAF*)

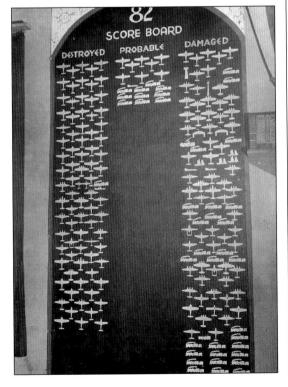

Capt Quince Brown poses in the cockpit of P-47D-21 42-25698 *Okie* at end of his first tour in June 1944. He would claim one more aerial success when he returned to combat with the 84th FS in late August (*USAAF*)

and Lt Donald DeVilliers, and Lt Robert Bosworth of the 82nd FS, were amongst those credited with 13 victories following their strafing run – two more were claimed by 78th HQ staffer, and ace, Lt Col Olin Gilbert. Lts Harold Beck and Wilbur Grimes of the 84th FS then hit a roundhouse full of locomotives at Conflans, in France, before finding an airfield nearby and destroying two Ju 88s and a Bf 109.

That afternoon 78A Group targeted railway marshalling yards at Sainte Menehold, Tagnon, Fagnières-Suippe and Épernay, where a train of 50 oil wagons was destroyed by exploding bombs. This success was tempered somewhat by the death of Lt Louis Dicks of the 82nd FS, whose P-47 was downed by light flak over Épernay.

The following day Lt Charles Parmelee of the 84th FS downed two Bf 109s northwest of Paris to take his tally to four kills overall.

On 12 August the 82nd FS destroyed five locomotives at Fournieres, in France, with the 83rd FS destroying two more and blowing up 35 oil wagons. The 84th FS topped both units, however, when its pilots set off a 20-wagon ammunition train, the explosion of which completely destroyed the railway yard at Breuil, also in France.

Attacking increasingly well-defended ground targets cost the 83rd FS the life of ace Capt Charles Peal on 14 August, his fighter last being seen bracketed by heavy flak after he had made his bombing run on a train near Noyon, in France. He had claimed the last four of his ten victories just 48 hours earlier during the devastating strafing attack on Château-Salins.

The 78th returned to escort duty on the 15th, shepherding one of the first daylight missions flown by RAF Bomber Command in more than two years. The 'heavies' targeted Deelen airfield, southeast of Amsterdam, and seven Lancasters and Halifaxes were lost to 88 mm flak.

On 27 August 78B Group found a marshalling yard at Metz full of trains and dropped two bombs that set off a sympathetic explosion of ammunition and fuel which demolished the target, and everything in it, sending a smoke column rising to 10,000 ft. Airfields at Thionville and Chatel-Chéhéry, both in France, were also attacked by the 82nd FS, with future ace Capt Richard Conner claiming one of three victories credited to the unit.

The group's high combat tempo continued on the evening of 28 August. During the second mission of the day, HQ staffer Maj Jack Oberhansly was leading the 82nd FS as top cover for the group's strafers, shooting up rolling stock near Charleroi, in Belgium, when he dove on a Ju 88 that he spotted on the deck heading northeast. Diving from 11,000 ft, he closed to within 50 yards of the bomber before he broke off his attack. The aircraft crashed into a field and blew up, thus providing Oberhansly with his sixth, and last, aerial kill. Fellow ace, and deputy group commander, Lt Col Olin Gilbert was not so lucky, however, being forced to belly in after being hit by flak near Charleroi. Quickly making contact with the Resistance, he returned to the UK two weeks later. 84th FS pilot Lt John Lacy also had to crash-land after wagons he was targeting blew up and damaged his P-47. Unlike Gilbert, he was immediately captured.

Just over an hour later, at 1915 hrs, 82nd FS CO Maj Joseph Myers, flying as 'Surtax Blue Leader', was providing top cover for the group, with newly-arrived 2Lt Wayne Coleman as his wingman. His element leader was 1Lt Fred Bolgert, who in turn had 2Lt Manfred Croy on his wing. Flying at 11,000 ft, they had just turned for home after covering a strafing mission to Termonde, near Brussels, when Myers spotted what he initially thought was a B-26 flying low over fields in the evening shadows near the Belgian village of Haaltert. He quickly realised that no Marauder could fly that fast, and called to Bolgert to follow with Croy as he dove to investigate, leaving Coleman as top cover. Myers pushed in war emergency power and water injection, registering 450 mph in a 45-degree dive and overhauled the stranger, which he finally recognised as a Me 262 jet.

The first of these mysterious aircraft had only been spotted by an Eighth Air Force pilot a month earlier. This particular Me 262A-1a, from 3./KG 51, was a bomber variant being evacuated by Ofw Hieronymous Lauer from the unit's base at Juvincourt, in France, to Ath-Chièvres, in Belgium. When Lauer had taken off the nose gear had failed to retract completely, which subsequently prevented him from flying at maximum speed at a much higher altitude.

From above, Coleman watched as Myers opened fire and missed;

'With tracers flying around him, the German was so low that he just put it onto the ground wheels-up in this open field. I saw the pilot get out and run for the trees, but then the three Thunderbolts made strafing runs. I told Maj Myers I was certain they had killed him.'

In fact Lauer had landed right outside Haaltert's cemetery, and he was able to hide among the trees. He was picked up by Wehrmacht troops later that night and returned to combat with KG 51. He was subsequently wounded in a fight with Thunderbolts from the 356th FG in October and then shot up while attacking the bridge at Remagen in March 1945.

In 1978 Coleman met Lauer after he had been tracked down by Fred Bolgert, who then corresponded with him. All three were guests at the dedication of the Resistance Museum in Haaltert. Myers' victory was the first by any Allied pilot over the new German jet. Over the years, several sources have named Quince Brown as the pilot responsible for this first kill of a German jet, but the two surviving members of the flight, as well as official group records, confirm that the victorious pilot was indeed Maj Myers, who went on to 'make ace'. Brown himself had only returned to the group from his 30-day leave on 28 August, taking command of the 84th FS.

August had been another eventful month for the 78th FG, with five enemy aircraft being shot down and 25 destroyed on the ground for the loss of five pilots killed in action, four captured and two evading.

On 6 July 1944, 2Lt Charles Parmelee's 84th FS flight pursued two fleeing Fw 190s over the Paris suburbs, where they were attacked by 15 more Focke-Wulfs. Parmelee and two others claimed Fw 190s shot down in the low altitude melee over the 'City of Light'. 'Making ace' on 1 September 1944, Charles Parmelee perished nine days later when he belly-landed his flak-damaged aircraft near Wiesbaden and slid into a hedge hiding a stone wall. The P-47 exploded and he was killed (*USAAF via John M Dibbs/Plane Picture Company*)

Maj Quince Brown claimed his final victory (a Bf 109 shot down near Liège-Trier) in P-47D-28 42-26567 on 1 September, just four days after returning to Duxford for a second tour of duty. On 6 September Brown fell victim to flak near Schleiden whilst flying P-47D-28 44-19569, and although he successfully bailed out, he was captured by German civilians and executed by two Waffen-SS soldiers (*USAAF*)

Brown soon got back into the swing of things, being one of five pilots credited with an aerial victory on 1 September. He was the only pilot in the 84th FS to claim a fighter shot down, near Liège-Trier, although fellow ace Lt Charles Parmelee was also credited with a strafing victory southwest of Antwerp. The remaining kills consisted of four Bf 110s caught overhead Gilze-Rijen airfield by the 83rd FS. The unit also lost two P-47s to flak, resulting in the death of Lt R N Jones. Flak claimed another aircraft on the 3rd and two on the 5th as the 78th continued to search out transport targets.

The pace of missions was such that by 6 September recently promoted Maj Quince Brown was already on his fifth mission of his second tour, leading 78A Group on a strafing attack on Vogelsang airfield, near Schleiden, in Germany. Capt Dick Hewitt led the 82nd FS as high cover for the mission, later recalling;

'I was at 8000 ft with my four flights, and had a good view of what happened when they hit the target. After one pass, Maj Brown chose to abandon the attack after being hit. He pulled away from the airfield, with the rest of the group behind him, and headed towards Schleiden. He must have figured that he might find a locomotive or two, since Schleiden was a rail centre. Once we were over the town, it was evident from the telltale smoke in the railway marshalling yard that we had found a good target.

'Maj Brown turned toward the smoke and started a pass at a train. Suddenly, the sky was full of 20 mm and 37 mm tracers all aimed at Brown's flight as a flak car embedded in the train immediately opened fire. As he started his pullout, I heard Brown call that he'd taken an engine hit and was bailing out. I saw his 'chute billow as it opened, but it was only a moment later that he hit the ground. Civilians from the nearby train and farmers in an adjoining field surrounded him almost immediately, giving him no chance to escape into nearby woods.'

At that point, other flak positions in the town opened up and the Thunderbolts turned for home.

The 78th was hard-hit by the loss of their leading ace, a man who was popular and admired by everyone – two pilots from the 83rd FS also fell to flak that day attacking airfields in Belgium.

After the war it was reported that Quince Brown had been shot by a German civilian, who was later executed in 1947 for the crime. This had not in fact been the case. In 2003, Dick Hewitt received a telephone call from Frank Guth of Schleiden, who was researching a book about the war as it had happened in his town. After repeating the long-accepted story about Brown being executed by a civilian, Guth informed Hewitt of what had really happened, as recounted to him by his aunt, who had been nine at the time.

The civilians who had surrounded Brown in the field brought him into Schleiden and had planned to turn him over to a Luftwaffe detachment in the town as a PoW. However, before this could happen, two Waffen-SS troops took Brown from the civilians. To their horror, one of the soldiers pulled out his pistol and shot Brown in the back of the head in the middle of the town square. After the war, this crime was reported to the American occupation authorities, and the two SS men were tracked down and arrested. In 1947 they were tried as war criminals for shooting a surrendered prisoner and duly executed.

The day before Brown's loss, Maj Robert Eby, one of the 78th FG's original pilots from February 1942 and most recently the group's operations officer, completed his tour. Promoted to lieutenant colonel, he was transferred to the 3rd Air Division HQ as Director of Fighter Operations. At last, the 78th had a 'friend at court' who would have a voice in their future combat assignments.

During the evening of 9 September the group made dive-bombing and strafing attacks on targets in the Giessen-Frankfurt-Fulda area of Germany at 1750 hrs. The 82nd FS's 'White Flight' shot up eight locomotives before becoming involved in a low-level fight with several Fw 190s.

At the same time, other flights hit the airfield at Giessen. As they made their run in, four Fw 190s managed to get airborne. Flying as No 4 in 'Yellow Flight', Lt Wayne Coleman spotted one of the German fighters as it tucked its gear up, hitting it from the rear – the pilot got out just before the aircraft nosed over and dove into the ground, exploding on impact. A second Fw 190 then came at Coleman from head-on, before breaking sharply left to avoid a collision. The fighter duly went into a spin and crashed. Coleman then spotted a third Fw 190 on the tail of a P-47 and closed in. He fired to distract the enemy pilot, who executed a sharp turn in Coleman's direction. The two protagonists went 'round a few turns' until the German realised he was losing and turned to run.

Engaging the water injection, Coleman chased the Fw 190 for five minutes before getting into range and hitting the wing root and cockpit area. The German fighter chandelled to 200 ft, rolled twice and went straight in, where it exploded on impact, the pilot apparently already dead. In his first aerial combat Coleman had scored a triple. His days as a wingman were soon over!

84th FS CO Maj Ben Mayo also scored multiple kills on 9 September to 'make ace' after strafing eight locomotives. Despite being low on ammunition, he went after eight Fw 190s he spotted 'on the deck' over Giessen, Diving on them from 7000 ft, Mayo determined to close to point-blank range before opening fire because he only had about 75 rounds remaining in four guns. Spotting an Fw 190 dropping behind the others, he hit it with two short bursts and the fighter crashed from 75 ft. Mayo then swung in behind a second fighter and started firing with his one operable machine gun. Hit in the belly, the Fw 190 began to trail smoke and then sharply climbed in a chandelle up to 1000 ft. The pilot then half-rolled and bailed out.

In a perfect example of the wingman's craft, Maj Mayo's No 2, Lt Wilbur Grimes, described his role in this engagement;

Capt Richard Hewitt flew an impressive 127 missions with the 82nd FS between August 1943 and VE Day, commanding the squadron on three separate occasions during this time. He finished the war with 8.333 victories to his credit, the bulk of these coming in the Thunderbolt in 1944. Note that Hewitt's P-47D-28 is equipped with a Curtiss Type-836 asymmetric paddle propellor, rather than the more common Curtiss Type-542 symmetrical paddle prop (*USAAF*)

'Maj Mayo, "White Leader", called out bogies on the deck heading east southeast near Butzbach. We came out of the sun at "six o'clock" and chased them east for 20 minutes full out. I was left of my leader, 90 degrees going toward him. An Fw 190 chandelled from right to left and got on my leader's tail. I threw my aeroplane into a 90-degree left bank, and allowing deflection, I set my sights on my leader's aeroplane and opened fire. I continued firing until I had to go under my leader's tail.

'Glancing up to the right to observe the enemy aircraft, I saw my strikes start at his canopy and go out to his right wingtip. His aeroplane did a violent snap to the right, changed direction 180 degrees and headed down about 25 ft off the deck out of control. I racked my aeroplane left to stay with my leader and lost sight of the enemy aircraft I had fired on, but Lt Dunham of the 82nd, shooting at the same aeroplane, hit the enemy pilot as he was bailing out and the aircraft exploded into a hill.'

The following day the group enjoyed one of its most successful missions of the war when, during a series of strafing attacks on airfields around Mannheim, its pilots claimed 38 aircraft (mainly Ju 88s and He 111s) destroyed at Mainbullau and Gernsheim. Top scorer was the 84th FS's Capt Raymond Smith, with fellow aces Lt R R Bonebrake, Maj J Myers, Capt R A Hewitt, Lt F E Harrington and Lt M R Capp also claiming victories. These successes came at a price, however, with three pilots being killed and two captured. Amongst the former was ace Lt Charles Parmelee, who perished when he belly-landed his flak-damaged aircraft near Wiesbaden and slid into a hedge hiding a stone wall. The P-47 exploded and he was killed.

There was hardly time to mourn the death of Quince Brown and any of the others before Lt Col Eby's transfer bore fruit and the 78th FG became involved in one of the most important events of the war in Europe – Operation *Market Garden*.

With the Wehrmacht having been effectively driven out of France by early September, there was optimism the war might be over by the end of the year. Field Marshal Bernard Montgomery, commanding the 21st Army Group, proposed a bold plan to utilise the First Allied Airborne Army to seize the three major bridges in Holland, with the final one at Arnhem providing an opportunity to bypass the defensive 'Siegfried Line' and get across the Rhine into Germany. Three airborne divisions, the US 82nd and 101st and the British 1st Airborne, would provide the striking force.

The plan suffered a major roadblock, however, in the person of Gen Lewis Brereton, the USAAF officer placed in command of the First Allied Airborne Army. Brereton and his staff refused to schedule more than one airlift a day for each division involved. This meant that there would be insufficient paratroopers available on the ground in Holland at the outset of the operation to overcome German opposition, and that vital re-supply missions to deliver additional troops would be spread over three days. Furthermore, it was decided that the re-supply missions would be flown in daylight due to the severe problems that beset the night drops at Normandy. Finally, the troop carriers would not fly close to Arnhem so as to avoid flak, which meant that British paratroops were dropped too far from their target bridge.

Thunderbolts of the 56th, 353rd and 78th Fighter Groups were assigned as escorts for the troop carrier aircraft and ground support for the invasion, flying alongside other fighter units from the Ninth Air Force based on the Continent.

At 1200 hrs on 17 September, Lt Col Joe Myers led the 78th along the routes to be taken by the incoming transports. As Lt Wayne Coleman later remembered, 'Our job was to go in before the transports got there and knock out the flak guns. Lt Col Myers sent one flight down to make a low pass. When they took fire, the rest of us attacked'. Dropping 260-lb

fragmentation bombs on the gun emplacements and following with strafing passes, the Thunderbolts spent nearly an hour working over the area, claiming the destruction of 16 multi-gun sites and damage to 37 others – a Bf 109 was also destroyed on the ground by ace Lt Herbert Shope at Gilze-Rijen. The units then provided close escort to the C-47s and their towed gliders. Ten Skytrains were lost to flak from guns the pilots of the 78th had failed to spot, however.

On 18 September, Lt Col Jack Oberhansly led the group in the late afternoon as they again escorted C-47s. Twelve light flak sites and a large truck convoy were put out of action before the weather closed in with a 500-ft cloud ceiling. Forced down into the light flak zone by the overcast conditions, the 78th lost five fighters to flak – one pilot was killed and four captured. Although these losses were significant, they were considerably lighter than the 14 P-47s lost by the 56th FG that same day. Poor weather on 19 September kept all fighters grounded, significantly boosting the efforts of the German troops defending Arnhem from attack by British paratroopers.

The 78th continued providing support on the 20th, unaware that surviving British paratroopers had begun to escape from the battle zone. On 23 and 25 September the group escorted re-supply missions flown to Nijmegen.

For its 237 sorties flown in support of the doomed British parachute assault on Arnhem, the 78th FG was awarded the Army Air Forces Distinguished Unit Citation. The 20 low-level missions during the month of September had resulted in the loss of 21 P-47s, with nine pilots being killed, ten captured, one evading and one being rescued from the Channel. The group had claimed 13 aerial victories, 47 strafing victories and the destruction of 80 locomotives.

October saw the 78th return to providing escort for heavy bombers over Germany, while fighter-bombing was left to the Ninth Air Force – a decision pilots at Duxford heartily welcomed after the carnage of the past four months. On the 7th Lt Col Myers led the group to Leipzig. At 1220 hrs Maj Richard Conner was warned by Fighter Control of approaching high-speed bogies. Spotting them at 14,000 ft, he quickly identified the aircraft as Me 262s. Conner led his flight

Immaculately presented P-47D-28 44-19566 *IRON ASS II* of deputy group CO and 7.666-victory ace Lt Col Jack Oberhansly was photographed at Duxford between missions in September 1944. He had claimed his final aerial victory (a Ju 88 near Charleroi) in this aircraft on 28 August 1944, having only returned from leave in the USA six days earlier (*USAAF*)

1Lt Huie Lamb of the 82nd FS used P-47D-25 42-28422 to down a Me 262 on 15 October 1944. Having spotted the jet near Osnabrück, he dived at maximum power with water-injection from 15,000 ft down to 4000 ft and engaged the fighter over Bohmte airfield. The Me 262 exploded on impact with the ground, and Lamb made his getaway at low altitude, considering himself lucky to have escaped the numerous flak batteries ringing the airfield. This was only the third Me 262 to be shot down by an VIII Fighter Command pilot, and the second credited to the 78th FG. Lamb had claimed his first kill in 42-28422 three days earlier, downing a Bf 109 over Hamburg. He subsequently 'made ace' flying the P-51 in 1945 (*USAAF*)

down from 24,000 ft but was unable to get close enough to the two jets to open fire. The Me 262s were short of fuel, however, and as they circled an airfield near Osnabrück in preparation for landing Conner caught them up and attacked. As the Me 262 pilot lowered his undercarriage Conner fired one quick shot from astern before overrunning the rapidly slowing jet in an effort to evade flak. His wingman saw the Me 262 crash.

Fellow aces Maj Myers and Lt Robert Bosworth also enjoyed success during the mission, downing a Bf 109 each over Leipzig.

Maj Conner claimed another aerial victory on 12 October when he destroyed an Fw 190 over Hamburg. Squadronmate (and future ace) 2Lt Huie Lamb claimed a Bf 109 kill during the same engagement.

A mission to Osnabrück three days later found more jets, most likely from *Kommando Nowotny* – the first Me 262 fighter unit to see combat. A flight of four long-nosed Fw 190Ds were chased providing cover for the jets over their airfield at Bohmte, and a fight quickly developed. Future 83rd FS ace Lt Robert Green, flying 'Cargo Red Three', spotted two Fw 190s and downed one of them, then engaged another one and destroyed it too with a 90-degree deflection shot. Four more then appeared on the scene and Green downed one of them as well. 'Circling up', he recalled, 'I saw a P-47 [flown by Lt J S Reems] fighting an Fw 190 on the deck and I told him I'd give him top cover. The enemy pilot was an old hand, doing half snap rolls, and the two were about even, so I decided to lend assistance. My first burst achieved many strikes on his fuselage, cockpit and engine, and his canopy shot off and he went in and exploded'.

A short while later former 'Yank in the RAF' Capt John Brown led his wingman 2Lt Huie Lamb on a fast strafing attack of a nearby marshalling yard. As they raced away from the defending flak batteries, Lamb spotted a Me 262 at 4000 ft;

'I called it in to John, but he didn't see it. He told me to go for it, and he would cover me. I was keeping track of the bogie, and dove at him. I was indicating over 500 mph as I closed. I knew they could outperform us, so I opened fire out of range, hoping to hit him, but all that did was warn him I was there. He started a turn away and I hit the water injection – the only time I ever used it – and picked up about 25 mph, which allowed

The first USAAF fighter to down a Me 262 was P-47D-25 42-27339, flown by Maj Joseph Myers of the 82nd FS. On 28 August 1944 he had spotted a twin-engined aircraft flying low near Termonde, in Belgium. Diving to investigate the contact, Myers quickly identified the aircraft as a Me 262. Just as Myers opened fire, the German pilot Ofw Lauer of 3./KG 51 made a wheels-up landing in a field. Myers also destroyed three He 111s with this machine during a strafing attack on Meinbullen airfield on 10 September and shot down a Bf 109 over Leipzig on 7 October. The fighter heads a line-up of 82nd FS machines at Bassingbourn airfield, which was the 78th FG's temporary home in November 1944 after heavy rain had turned Duxford's runway into a quagmire (*USAAF*)

me to close on him. He was turning wide, and I opened fire again and hit him in the forward fuselage. He flipped over then straightened out and went lower. I closed in to around 100 ft right behind him. I only had two inner guns that still had ammo after the strafing. I hit his left engine and he fell off to the right and went in, exploding on impact.'

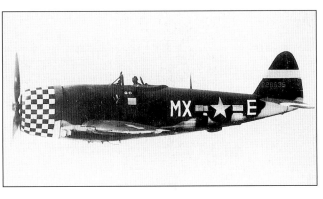

As flak tracers started flying around him, Lamb realised that his foe had led him into a flak corridor right over the airfield at Bohmte. 'I'd been so close to him that they couldn't open fire before, but as soon as he went in, every gun on that field opened up on me! I got hit in the rudder, and it jammed for a minute. John radioed me to go lower, and I went across that field – at maximum speed so low I must have nearly hit the ground with my prop. It was all a blur. I got out of there and pulled up. John joined up and told me that I had taken a lot of hits. This was my second victory, and I had previously promised myself that I would do a victory roll whenever I claimed a kill. However, with my P-47 so badly shot up, I decided I'd just worry about getting back on the ground in one piece, which is what I did.'

The 82nd and 83rd FSs had claimed eight aerial victories on 15 October for the loss of one P-47 to flak, its pilot being captured.

Early autumn rains, which presaged the worst European winter in a century, then set in. Things soon got so bad at Duxford that operations were severely restricted from its grass runway. On 26 October, for example, two P-47s were unable to depart on a mission after they became stuck in mud while awaiting their turn to take off. By month-end the group had lost just two pilots in combat (one of whom was a PoW), while scoring 13 aerial victories, one strafing victory and 24 locomotives destroyed in 17 missions.

The rains that continued into early November turned Duxford's runway into a quagmire, making it too soft and muddy for flight operations with fully loaded P-47s. Aircraft were swiftly moved to the 91st BG's base at Bassingbourn, 14 miles west of Duxford. With the Thunderbolts gone, US Army engineers began to lay down a 3500 ft by 150 ft pierced-steel-planking runway between two areas of steel matting that had been laid down at either end of the airfield, giving 4100 ft of useable runway.

Col Gray summoned the group to a meeting on 16 November at Duxford's base theatre, where he announced that the P-47s would depart at the end of the month, to be replaced by P-51D Mustangs. This move was almost universally condemned by pilots and groundcrew alike. Pilots had grown to love their P-47s since their entry into service at Duxford in the spring of 1943, respecting the fighter's higher survivability rate in the kinds of missions they had been flying in comparison with the Mustang – its liquid-cooled Merlin engine did not cope well with flak damage. The only good thing conceded to the P-51D/K was its greater range, which would now allow the group to escort bombers on any given mission. Groundcrews did not relish having only a few weeks to learn a completely new aircraft that they would have to maintain in the open in the middle of winter.

P-47D-25 42-26635 has been well known to aviation enthusiasts for the past 70 years due to a series of identification shots that were taken of the aircraft during an air-to-air photography session flown by future ace Capt Richard Hewitt in August 1944. This sortie was specially arranged so that the group photographer could record the new RAF Dark Green/Sky camouflage being applied to all P-47s in the 78th FG. 42-26635 has been regularly credited as being Hewitt's aeroplane by many historians, but the ace maintains 'it was just an aeroplane I flew for this photo session'. RAF Dark Green was an almost-exact match for pre-1943 USAAF Olive Drab, since both were based on the official formulation for World War 1 RAF PC10 camouflage paint. All Eighth Air Force groups used RAF paint in 1944 due to the unavailability of stocks from the USA at that time (*USAAF*)

Maj Richard Conner (second from the right) was CO of the 82nd FS from 28 August to 2 December 1944, during which time he claimed 4.5 aerial and 2.5 strafing kills. Starting a second tour in February 1945, again as CO of the 82nd, he assumed this position in the 84th FS after its CO of five days, Maj Harry Downing, was shot down by a Bf 109 over Osnabrück on 19 March. Connor only lasted 48 hours in his new job, for he fell to flak while strafing airfields near Dresden. Crash-landing in no-man's land between German and Soviet lines, Conner managed to make contact with Red Army units and eventually ended up in Moscow. He returned to Duxford on 10 May 1945 (*USAAF*)

The first mission from Bassingbourn was not flown until 21 November due to bad weather, 78A Group rendezvousing with the bombers over Nordholz and then heading for Hamburg. Leading 'Black Flight' of the 82nd FS, Capt Richard Hewitt spotted 15 Bf 109s forming up for an attack near Hanover. He hit a fighter that went straight in from 4000 ft, while Lt Allen Rosenblum fought another Bf 109 for ten minutes before being able to send it spinning in flames all the way to the ground. Staff pilot Capt Robert Holmes spotted another Bf 109 on Maj Richard Conner's tail and sent it earthward with a dead pilot at the controls, while Conner himself forced the pilot to bail out of a Messerschmitt he had been chasing. Turning into the others, he then shot down a second with two bursts to 'make ace'. On the way home the squadron strafed the aerodrome at Gütersloh, in Germany, destroying two aircraft there but losing a P-47 to flak.

On 25 November, during an escort to Koblenz, pilots saw the launching of their first V2s. Indeed, one of the three they spotted was so close that they could see it rise to 30,000 ft before the missile accelerated into outer space on its way to England. The next day saw 78B Group provide penetration-target withdrawal support for the 1st BD's mission to Osnabrück, in Germany. Again, the 82nd FS scored when it was vectored onto 40 Bf 109s approaching the bombers over Rheine. Lt Donald Hart engaged the enemy fighters first when he hit a Bf 109 in its engine, while Flt Off Harold Liebenrood caught another from 'six-o'clock' and set it afire. Lt Manfred Croy chased a third machine down to low level, where it burst into flames under the weight of his fire and crashed.

82nd FS ace Capt John Hockery led his flight against another formation of Bf 109s that broke through the escorts towards the bombers;

'Spotted 30+ ME109s attacking the bombers and I led my flight into them. I caught one in a deflection shot, getting strikes on his canopy and wing roots. Pieces came off and I fired again. Then he flamed and went down. I spotted another 109 with *staffelkapitän* chevrons on its side and followed him to the deck. He led me to an airdrome, where we did a Lufbery at 1500 ft right over the field. They were throwing up lots of flak, but I stayed on the enemy. All of a sudden there was a big explosion on the 109 and his wing came off, flicking him into the ground. I think his own flak shot him down.

'I broke off for home, then started to climb into a fight above, when three FW190s passed me coming down. Getting into a rat race with them, they turned out to be better pilots than I had expected. My water-injection ran out and they started to catch me, so I turned on them to fight it out. Just as I got strikes all over one of them, an explosion behind me blew off part of my wing and I crashed into a field. I got out and hid in a ditch as two FW190s strafed my wrecked P-47. I was made a PoW shortly thereafter.'

As all this was going on, future 83rd FS aces Capts Robert Bonebrake and Harold Barnaby both claimed victories, the former downing an Fw 190 south of Dummer Lake with two bursts and the latter an unidentified aircraft during a strafing pass on Weissewarte airfield. Finally, the 84th FS was also credited with single aerial and strafing successes.

November ended with four losses (two pilots killed and two captured) in combat in return for 13 aerial victories, six strafing kills and 47 locomotives destroyed.

COMING OF THE MUSTANG

The onset of poor weather meant that the 78th FG would not engage the enemy again until 19 December, three days after the first Mustangs had arrived at Duxford for the 82nd FS. Pilots initially checked out in a handful of war-weary P-51Bs that had been brought in first.

'Fighter pilots are creatures of habit, and most everyone in the 78th agreed they wouldn't give up flying the P-47 for anything in the world', recalled 1Lt Frank Oiler. 'We had been warned that the change was coming, and all the pleading and complaining in the world didn't change a thing. Even though we dug in our heels, they began to pull our P-47s from our icy cold fingers and ferry them to the Ninth Air Force from mid-December. We received what felt to us like a demotion in aeroplanes – Mustangs. Our brothers in the 56th FG must have had all the luck in the Air Force, as they got to keep their Jugs!'

Wayne Coleman remembered an item of importance to a pilot;

'The P-51B's cockpit was smaller and tighter than the P-47. In the winter, all bundled up in fleece-lined flying suit over a wool uniform and long johns, with flying boots and flying gloves on, we filled up the Mustang's cockpit. I made sure I always answered nature's call before I went flying, but one time I was surprised to hear from her while I was at 10,000 ft. It took ten minutes to get down through all the layers to use the relief tube, and halfway through it froze up and by the time the overflow reached me, it was damn cold!'

19 December saw the last big combat mission flown by the 78th FG with the P-47, which still equipped the 83rd and 84th FSs. With calls for urgent support from beleaguered Allied troops in the face of the all-out Wehrmacht assault during the Battle of the Bulge, which had been raging in the Ardennes under the cover of poor weather since 16 December, the 78th was the only Eighth Air Force fighter unit to get airborne in the atrocious conditions.

The bombers' target was Trier, and shortly after the 'heavies' had dropped their ordnance a warning came of incoming fighters but nothing was spotted in the cloudy skies, so the P-47 squadrons strafed a train after aborting an attack on Babenhausen airfield. As they withdrew, pilots from the 83rd FS spied 30 Bf 109s and set off after them. Moments later the squadron was engaged by 20 Fw 190D-9s. As future ace Lt John Kirk fired at a Bf 109 that went straight in, an Fw 190 engaged him. Outturning his opponent at just 300 ft, Kirk watched as the 'Dora-9' pilot suddenly bailed out. Lt Francis Harrington, who also subsequently became an ace, hit a Bf 109 that had turned to engage him – it went straight in inverted. Harrington then went after three Fw 190s, firing at one that dove away. Giving chase, he hit it again and the fighter burst into flames, mowing down trees and starting a forest fire as it hit the ground.

Pilots from the 78th FG play up for the camera as they 'resist' transitioning from their beloved P-47 to the P-51 in December 1944. The fighter that these unfortunate individuals are being dragged towards is war weary P-51B-5 43-6593, which had previously served with the 352nd FG's 487th FS as *Brutal Lulu*. It was the mount of 5.5-victory ace Lt Robert Berkshire, who claimed four aerial victories and a solitary strafing kill in the Mustang between 9 April and 30 May 1944. Note how muddy the airfield is – the fighters are parked on steel matting. Also worth noting is the flat finish of the veteran Mustang in comparison with the high-gloss Thunderbolt (*USAAF via John M Dibbs/Plane Picture Company*)

Capt Robert Bonebrake also enjoyed success during the engagement, downing one of three Bf 109s that he got into a fight with. He then destroyed an Fw 190 too. The final kill in this one-sided clash went to Capt Frank Fish, who chased four Bf 109s and hit one that blew up after the pilot had bailed out.

Fog closed in over East Anglia until 28 December, when Col Fred Gray led P-47s from the 84th FS on an uneventful escort to Koblenz. The following day the group was divided into three formations. First off at 0940 hrs was the 84th FS, which put up 32 P-47s as 78C Group, while 78A and B Groups consisted of 32 P-51D/Ks from the 82nd and 83rd FSs on their first mission with the new fighter. The Thunderbolts went to Malmedy, in Belgium, while the Mustangs escorted bombers to Frankfurt.

The 82nd FS's Huie Lamb, newly-promoted to captain, had a very close call;

'We as a group were not that knowledgeable about dealing with technical difficulties with the aeroplane at that time, which may have led to my problem. I was element lead, with John Chiles as my wingman. As we approached Frankfurt, John's radio went out and he aborted, which meant I had to return with him. We flew out over Holland at 25,000 ft. As we passed the coastal flak belt, we let down to 20,000 ft. Suddenly my temperature gauge started climbing. I was on automatic control and went to manual control, then opened the radiator door and the temperature came back into the green arc. I closed the door and continued on.

'We were crossing the North Sea to a landfall at Orford Ness, in Suffolk. About halfway there, the temperature went into the yellow, close to the red arc. I opened the radiator door again, but this time it had no effect. I throttled back, hoping to make it to the coast, but the engine overheated and caught fire. I unfastened my shoulder harness to bail out and slid the canopy back, but it jammed. When I finally got it open I was too low. I was going to have to ditch, and all I now had on was the seatbelt.

'I slowed, dropped flaps and used the surface chop to head into the wind. I was stalled out just as I touched down, but my left wingtip hit first and I cartwheeled. I hit the gunsight and broke a tooth and cut my

P-51D-20 44-63712 *FLY'N TIME BOMB*
was assigned to Maj Ray Smith of
the 84th FS. Its nickname was a 'tip
of the hat' from the personnel of
the 84th FS to the many mechanical
problems and accidents experienced
by the group during its troubled
transition to the Mustang during
the bitter winter of 1944/45. Smith
served with the 84th from October
1943 through to April 1945, and
claimed his solitary aerial victory and
five strafing kills flying the P-47 in
1944. Note also the impressive tally
of locomotives destroyed that adorns
44-63712 (*USAAF*)

lip pretty badly. The aeroplane quickly came to a stop, and I stood up to
get my dinghy. The water in the cockpit was quickly up to my knees and
the aeroplane was sinking fast. I threw the dinghy out and inflated my
Mae West, and got out just as the P-51 went down.

'The water was really cold – they told me later it was 40°F. I inflated
the dinghy, but I couldn't get in before it floated away. John Chiles saw
my predicament, but he couldn't radio for help. We didn't know it at the
time, but John Crump from the 357th FG just happened to be doing an
air test at the same time and he saw me go in and radioed a Mayday.

'John Chiles flew to Martlesham Heath and saw a Walrus taxiing to the
runway – they were responding to Crump's Mayday so they were ready to
go. John landed and told them he would lead them to me. He said it seemed
to take forever for the Walrus to get off, and he then had to circle to stay
with it. He flew to where I was, and circled until the Walrus landed, then
had to leave since he was almost out of gas. The Walrus aircrewman had a
hell of a time pulling me out, since my clothes were waterlogged and I was
close to being unconscious from exposure. They shut down the engine so
they could pull me in through the rear hatch, then they had trouble getting
it started, but finally they managed to take off. Twenty minutes later they
had me in the hospital – I was suffering from exposure. When I came to,
the doctor told me my body temperature had been so low when I got there
that had I been in the water another five minutes I would likely have died.'

Lamb was one of the few pilots in the Eighth Air Force to successfully
ditch a Mustang in the Channel and survive.

30 December saw the 84th FS put up 32 P-47s that were vectored onto
several 'enemy' formations over the frontline that ultimately turned out to
be Allied aircraft. The 82nd and 83rd FSs sent 35 P-51s, led by Lt Col Myers,
as escorts for bombers targeting communications sites in western Germany.

The group's final mission of 1944 was also its last with the P-47, Capt
Pat Maxwell leading 13 Thunderbolts on a freelance fighter sweep to the
Hamburg area. After being vectored around Bremen, Hanover and Dummer
Lake without finding anything, the pilots turned for home. Spotting a train
below, Maxwell led his wingman on a strafing run but he was going too fast
and had to pull out of the attack, having only damaged it. Climbing back
up to 2500 ft, he then spotted a lone Fw 190 at 1500 ft;

'I called him off and peeled after him. My closure was very fast from
dead astern. He spotted me and broke up to the left. I put the dot on the

canopy and opened fire from 400 yards, with 80 degrees deflection. His belly tank blew up and he flipped over and fell like a rock. The pilot tried to bail out at 200 ft but his chute opened just as he hit the ground.'

Maxwell landed from his last mission of his second tour, and the final mission of a 78th FG squadron in the Thunderbolt, to be awarded a silver beer mug by Col Gray honouring the group's 400th victory – the last to be scored in a P-47. The group closed out the final month of the momentous year of 1944 with no pilot losses, eight aerial victories and a locomotive destroyed.

Converting to the Mustang proved particularly tricky with the onset of extreme weather conditions in eastern England in the new year. For example, on 8 January the first big snowstorm to hit East Anglia since the Eighth Air Force arrived in the UK resulted in five P-51s being ground-looped on takeoff on the icy plank runway. The mission was immediately cancelled. By then, the group had also lost three Mustangs, although only one of these was due to enemy action. The first had crashed near Saarbrücken, in Germany, on 2 January following mechanical failure, the second had been flown into a smokestack in fog and the third had been downed by flak.

The group's first victories with the Mustang, and only aerial successes that month, came on 14 January near Cologne when 82nd FS pilot Lt Willard Warren and his wingman Lt William DeGain spotted 14 fighters at low altitude. Diving from 26,000 ft, both pilots went through a second formation of 15 they had failed to spot in their pursuit of their foes. Warren caught an Fw 190, killing its pilot with his first burst and watching as the fighter flick-rolled into the ground. Seeing that his leader's tail was clear, DeGain moved up and hit a Bf 109, whose pilot bailed out. In a reversal of roles, Warren then shot an Fw 190 off DeGain's tail with a deflection shot – it crashed and exploded. Squadronmate Lt Robert Smith played 'hide-and-seek' with a Bf 109 in clouds over Cologne, sending it down to crash into a three-gun flak battery.

Maj Leonard Marshall of the 84th FS, leading 78C Group, spotted what he thought at first were three 'bogies' but they turned out to be a P-51 chasing two Bf 109s. As Marshall closed on one of the enemy fighters its pilot broke left and tried to belly in, only for his aircraft to explode upon hitting the ground. Marshall turned his attention to the remaining Bf 109, which was engaged in combat with squadronmate Lt Louis Hereford. The two Mustang pilots made quick work of the remaining enemy fighter.

The 84th's Lt Richard Spooner led his flight into an engagement with 20 Bf 109s that were trying to form up for an attack on B-17s of the 1st AD, shooting down one. Chasing another, he ran out of ammunition as he closed to within 100 ft of his target. His opponent was so spooked that he broke right and hit power lines, somersaulting into the ground. Frank Oiler, who was part of Spooner's flight, reported;

'We dropped our tanks and split-essed down on them. Rainbow Squadron split up the gaggle and Turquoise Squadron [Oiler was "Turquoise Yellow Three"] attacked them as they divided up into twos and threes. An Fw 190 went between my wingman and I, so I turned on his tail but lost him, then picked up a Me 109 and two Fw 190s being

1Lt Frank Oiler joined the 84th FS in June 1944 and commenced operations two months later. Initially reluctant to give up his P-47 when the 78th FG started replacing its Thunderbolts with the P-51D Mustang in December 1944, Oiler quickly became a believer in the new fighter when he shot down an Fw 190 and damaged a Bf 109 over Cologne on 14 January 1945 (*USAAF via John M Dibbs/Plane Picture Company*)

chased by a P-51. I called the P-51 to take one, and my wingman and I took the other. The Fw 190s broke in opposite directions and the Me 109 went straight up. I got in a Lufbery with one Fw 190 at 1100 ft, and by use of flaps I got on his tail in two turns. I got in a three-second burst at 35 degrees deflection, observed many strikes in the cockpit and he did a half snap and went in upside down.'

Squadronmate Lt Willis Lutz was heading home after finding his guns would not work. Spotting three aircraft, which he identified as Mustangs, he dropped down to join up with them, only to discover they were in fact Fw 190s! He then saw three more coming down on him, so he tried to sneak away. They had soon closed on the P-51, however, so Lutz tried his guns again, and this time they worked. He quickly set one of the Fw 190s on fire, before 'closing the circle' with a second Focke-Wulf and hitting it with a deflection shot that caused the machine's wings to burst into flames. The fighter rolled onto its back at 100 ft and crashed. Two more Fw 190s then came at Lutz, but he managed to out-turn them. After two more bursts he was out of ammunition, although by then one of his opponents had disengaged. He bluffed the second by pretending to make a firing pass, then broke for home.

As Lutz crossed Allied lines, he was hit by friendly fire and his engine caught fire. Lutz bailed out and was picked up by American troops.

A second escort mission later that same day saw 'Red Flight' of the 83rd FS bounce four Fw 190s over Diepholz airfield. Capt Peter Caulfield shot down one of them to bring the day's score to 14. With this, the Duxford pilots finally decided that they liked the P-51D after all.

Col Gray left at the end of January to become Director of Fighter Operations at Eighth Air Force HQ, his deputy commander, Lt Col Olin Gilbert, being promoted to take over the group. Ace Lt Col Joe Myers in turn became deputy commander.

In 19 missions in January the group had scored 14 aerial victories (all claimed on the 14th), destroyed 21 locomotives and lost four P-51s in combat and had a further eight written off due to engine failures or accidents caused by poor weather. Four pilots had been killed, three captured and one had evaded.

P-51D-20 44-63209 *Sherman Was Right!* (a reference to Union Gen W T Sherman's Civil War statement, 'All war is hell') was flown by 1Lt Frank Oiler of the 84th FS from January 1945. He claimed one aerial and two strafing kills in this machine, which was subsequently written off on 4 March when Lt Louis Hereford became lost in bad weather southeast of Nordlingen, in Germany, and was killed when the fighter crashed (*USAAF via John M Dibbs/ Plane Picture Company*)

Lt Col John Landers replaced Col Gray as group CO on 22 February 1945, the former having first seen combat as long ago as April 1942 in the Pacific. An ace against the Japanese, Landers claimed a further five aerial and five strafing victories in the ETO with the 55th and 357th FGs in 1944. Completing his second combat tour in December of that year, Landers spent two months on leave in the USA, before joining the 78th FG. Promoted to full colonel in May 1945, he is seen here posing with his P-51D-20 44-72218 shortly after VE Day. Landers claimed 3.5 aerial kills and 15 strafing victories in this fighter between 2 March and 16 April 1945 (*USAAF*)

On 3 February 1945 the 78th finally made it to Berlin, escorting bombers over the target. With no opposition, group leader Maj Harry Downing gave permission for pilots to break up and search out targets of opportunity during the return flight. The 84th FS discovered a fully packed airfield at Lüneburg whose flak batteries were not caught napping – the Mustang pilots flew into a wall of tracer. Two went down and were captured, while the rest found safety in the low cloud ceiling that allowed them to quickly elude the flak on pull-up after strafing. Despite the hostile reception, the 84th left 16 German aircraft burning.

22 February saw the 78th FG participate in Operation *Clarion*, which was an all-out aerial assault on the German road and rail network. Group CO Col Gilbert was joined by former 78th FG boss Col Fred Gray in a two-group sweep, shooting up rail targets across western Germany.

Upon returning to Duxford pilots met their new commanding officer, Lt Col John D Landers. Landers had made ace over New Guinea in December 1942 whilst flying P-40Es with the 49th FG. His second tour, in 1944, was in the ETO with the P-38-equipped 55th FG and the 357th FG, where he flew Mustangs – he scored an additional five aerial and five strafing victories with these groups. Returning for an unprecedented third tour, Landers was sent to the 78th FG.

Missions now almost always involved strafing, resulting in a growing list of pilot casualties. Indeed, the 78th went through more replacement pilots in the four months it saw action in 1945 than throughout 1944. February was a particularly bad month, with 15 P-51s being lost between the 20th and 28th. The worst day of all was 24 February, when four P-51s were hit by flak whilst strafing. Lt Edwin Anderson of the 82nd FS was the only pilot to survive being shot down, albeit as a PoW.

A mission to Berlin on 26 February saw Flt Off Charles O'Brien of the 83rd FS forced down in enemy territory with mechanical failure. Squadronmate Lt Leonard Olson was shot down minutes later attempting to land and pick him up. Although both men were captured, O'Brien was later shot and killed trying to escape.

On 27 February future ace Lt John Kirk was hit while strafing a train; 'All of a sudden, my right wing exploded and flipped the aeroplane on its side. I managed to level out just over the trees. The wing was still on but the aeroplane was vibrating badly. The gun covers were blown off and the ammunition belts were flapping at the trailing edge of the wing, which was bent. I started a climb so I could bail out at 1000 ft, but the P-51 was still flying so I climbed up to 2500 ft. Once there I decided that I would go as far as I could, maybe getting as far as France. My compass was out, so I started flying towards the setting sun. I asked on the radio if someone could turn to the sun and give me a heading, and once I had received this I put it into my gyrocompass. I was cruising fast to keep the P-51 aloft, and soon reached the coast.

'Chancing my luck, I headed on across the Channel and eventually reached home. I then made a practice landing on a cloud and discovered that my stalling speed was very high – 130 mph. Nevertheless, I brought it in "hot" and made a good landing.'

Kirk's crew chief subsequently found that a 20 mm shell had hit the lower wing, severing the main spar.

Eighteen missions had been flown in February, with six pilots killed in action, seven captured (one of whom was then killed) and four evading. The Luftwaffe had been conspicuous by its virtual absence in the air, with just two Me 262s being credited as probables and a third damaged. Sixteen strafing victories were claimed at Lüneburg on 3 February, however, and a record 103 locomotives destroyed during the course of the month.

March began badly, for on the 1st, following an uneventful escort, the group sought targets of opportunity north of Lake Constance. South of Stuttgart, Lt Ernest Boehner of the 82nd FS took a flak hit and went in, exploding on impact. A strafing run at Böblingen airfield a short while later saw flak down Lt Roy Higgins of the 84th FS. He too was killed. Finally, strafing a vehicle convoy near Heimsheim, Lt William Townsend, also of the 84th, hit the ground with the wingtip of his Mustang, which cartwheeled in and exploded.

Lt Col Landers led the 83rd FS as escorts for the 2nd AD's 2 March mission to Magdeburg. Between Berlin and the target, 24 Bf 109s were spotted at 15,000 ft as they formed up over Burg airfield for an attack on the 'heavies' – this was the first time the 78th had seen a formation of enemy fighters in the air since 14 January.

Landers led his pilots around to attack from out of the sun, but the German flight leaders were experienced and aggressive, dropping their tanks on spotting the oncoming P-51s. The remaining enemy aviators were novices, however, as they kept their centreline tanks. Most hastily bailed out after being shot at once or twice, and at one point nine parachutes were counted in the air. Landers was credited with two Bf 109s destroyed, as was his wingman Lt Jack Hodge. Back at Duxford, Landers termed all four victories 'freaks', as their opponents seemed more than happy to bail out whenever fired upon – ironically, Landers had struggled with faulty guns throughout this engagement.

Capt Foy Higginbottom, Maj William Julian and Lts Richard Kuehl and Hubert Davis all downed a Bf 109 each, while future ace Lt Duncan McDuffie got two, dropped below a solid undercast and scored a third, then chased a fourth through the clouds before sending it down too. The 83rd FS came home with 13 aerial victories for the loss of Lt Henry Staub, who became a PoW. He was the first pilot from the 78th to be shot down by the Luftwaffe since Lt Troy Eggleston on 26 November 1944.

1Lt John Kirk suffered engine failure in his P-51D-20 44-63620 *SMALL BOY HERE* shortly after VE Day, the ten-victory ace force landing near Duxford. Although he only flew 49 missions between October 1944 and war's end, Kirk had a highly successful tour with the 78th FG that saw him survive the conflict as the group's sixth-ranking ace. The majority of his kills were claimed in this aircraft between 19 March and 16 April 1945 (*USAAF*)

P-51D-25 44-64147 *BIG DICK* (the name refers to a throw in 'Acey-Deucy') was the final mount of 82nd FS CO Maj Dick Hewitt. In this photograph, taken by group intelligence officer Maj William Vincent, 'Black Flight' leader Capt Wayne Coleman (who claimed four aerial victories) is at the controls of *BIG DICK* as he escorts the unarmed two-seat P-51D that Hewitt flew on the Prague mission of 16 April 1945. The 78th FG destroyed 135 German aircraft on five Prague-area airfields – an Eighth Air Force record – and was awarded a second Distinguished Unit Citation for this mission. 'Black Flight' did not participate in the strafing, although Hewitt did destroy a Me 262 on the ground with this aircraft in the same area the following day for his final kill (*USAAF*)

Poor weather, mechanical failures and flying accidents resulted in the group losing seven Mustangs between 4 and 17 March, with four pilots being killed, two evading and one being plucked from the Channel.

On 19 March the 78th flew freelance withdrawal support for the 3rd AD's mission to Ruhland. As the formation crossed the German border, a pair of Me 262s made feint attacks to force the USAAF fighters to drop their tanks. The latter then kept the jets at bay by turning into them. As the 82nd FS approached Osnabrück, Capt Dick Hewitt spotted four Bf 109s at 8000 ft that he initially mistook for Spitfires. He bounced the quartet of Messerschmitts, only to spot many more enemy aircraft heading his way. The 82nd had stumbled on a large formation of fighters from IV./JG 27 that were forming up prior to intercepting the bombers. Hewitt called for assistance as he charged into the enemy fighters, whose pilots gave no appearance of wanting to run.

Jettisoning his wing tanks without switching fuel tanks, Hewitt was momentarily surprised when his engine cut out. He immediately rectified this problem, regained power and pulled in behind a Bf 109, whose pilot bailed out after several bursts of fire. Hewitt claimed a second Messerschmitt kill moments later. Simultaneously, his element leader, Lt Walter Bourque, climbed after four more Bf 109s, before turning on one that dived on him. This machine blew up under solid hits. In the meantime, Capt Huie Lamb spotted several more Bf 109s at a lower altitude;

'Just as I was closing in on the 109s, I glanced over my shoulder and there were four 190s diving on us! It was a trap. I was flying a P-51 that wasn't mine, the fighter being fitted with tail warning radar – its light was flashing red on my instrument panel! The radar warning light would go on and off, and I figured it was my wingman. I assumed that he was doing a pretty good job of staying with me. I made several head-on passes with the 109s, hitting one of them, before I called the rest of my flight to tell them it was time to head home. It was only then that I realised I was alone, and those radar warnings had been for German fighters on my tail! I climbed away and got the hell out of there myself.'

His squadronmate Lt Allen Rosenblum had become embroiled in a turning fight with a Bf 109 at just 400 ft. Flak drove him off the fighter's tail, at which point he spotted a lone Ar 234 jet bomber trying to flee the scene, which he attacked with Lt James Parker. The Arado soon struck a farmhouse and exploded. Re-forming, the two pilots made passes at ten Bf 109s until Rosenblum's tail warning radar went off. Looking behind him, he spotted 12 Fw 190s closing fast! Breaking into them, Rosenblum went head-to-head with one, which took hits and crashed into the ground below. Parker hit another of the Fw 190s with a 90-degree deflection shot, sending it down in flames.

Capt Winfield Brown destroyed yet another Bf 109, after which he formed up with Capt Huie Lamb. The two then discovered another Ar 234 that had made the mistake of heading for Osnabrück at the wrong time. It too was despatched by the Mustang pilots, crashing in flames into trees.

82nd FS pilot Lt Austin Miller attacked two Bf 109s, one of which rolled over and exploded. Moments later he fired at another one from long range – it caught fire and went straight in. Squadronmate Lt Ivan Keatley also downed a pair of Bf 109s. Element leader Lt Edwin Schneider attacked a Messerschmitt head-on, his quarry rolling twice before hitting the ground.

Answering Capt Hewitt's call for help, Lt Col Landers, who was once again leading the group, caught a Bf 109 as it split-essed out of the fight, while his element leader, Lt Howard Seeley of the 83rd FS, out-turned two more Messerschmitts in quick succession and shot them both down. Squadronmates Capt Foy Higginbottom and his wingman Lt Richard Kuehl shared a Bf 109, while ace Lt John Kirk chased an experienced enemy pilot before catching him as he reversed his turn – the fighter speared into the ground.

Staff pilot Maj Charles Christ went after a Bf 109 he spotted chasing a P-51 and hit it at close range, causing the pilot to bail out. Lt Hubert Davis of the 83rd FS bounced another Messerschmitt whose pilot bailed out after only a few strikes. Joining up with the unit's 'Yellow Flight', he came up behind a second Bf 109 whose pilot abandoned his fighter before Davis had had the chance to open fire!

Lt Peter Klassen, who was leading the 83rd FS on this occasion, climbed through a thin layer of cloud after spotting four contrails. He hit a Bf 109 whose pilot jettisoned his canopy but failed to bail out. Squadronmate Lt Robert Talbot also downed a Bf 109 a short while later, while future ace Lt Anthony Colletti fired at two Fw 190s that flew across the nose of his P-51. He hit one of them, its pilot immediately bailing out.

Maj Harry Downing led the 84th FS into the fight, shooting down a Bf 109 and an Fw 190 before he fell victim to the wingman of the latter aircraft – he bailed out to become a PoW. Element leader Lt William DeGain spotted eight Fw 190s as they bounced a flight of P-51s and shot one of them down. Three of the fighters then turned on him, and he only managed to get away by ducking into a cloud. The unit's 'Red Flight' chased four Bf 109s to the deck and destroyed three of them, future ace Lt Henry Slack bagging one. At the same time 'Blue Flight Lead', Lt Paul Ostrander, hit a Bf 109 whose pilot bailed out, while element leader Lt James Moores nailed one of three Fw 190s he caught at low altitude over an airfield.

When the Intelligence Officers at Duxford completed debriefings and compiled claims, the 78th had achieved one of the biggest single mission scores in Eighth Air Force history during the best day for the group in terms of aerial successes. No fewer than 32 aircraft had been shot down and 14 damaged, for the loss of two pilots killed and three captured.

On 21 March Maj Richard Conner led 43 Mustangs on a

Although not an ace, Lt Walter Bourque of the 82nd FS still claimed three victories and two damaged in March and April 1945. The most significant of these was the Me 262 he shot down on 21 March 1945 shortly after it had taken off from Giebelstadt (*USAAF*)

Lt Walter Bourque used P-51D-20 44-15745 to claim all of his successes. Flying as element lead to 82nd FS CO Capt Dick Hewitt, Bourque scored his first victory on 19 March 1945 when the 78th discovered 125 Bf 109s gathering for an attack on the bomber formation the group was escorting. Two days later he shot down a Me 262 from a formation of four that he attacked. Finally, on 10 April, Bourque destroyed a Bf 109 on the ground at Werder airfield. Note the 110-gallon metal drop tanks fitted to the Mustang, which were only used by the Eighth Air Force at the very end of the war (*USAAF*)

Squadronmates 1Lt William Spengler (left) and Capt Harold Barnaby (centre) of the 83rd FS share a joke for the camera in front of the former's P-51D-25 44-72481 *Buzzin' Cuzzin* in April 1945. Barnaby, who claimed four aerial victories and a solitary strafing kill to 'make ace', also downed a Me 262 on 22 March 1945. A veteran of 106 missions with the 78th between February 1943 and April 1945, Barnaby scored four of his five kills in the Thunderbolt (*USAAF*)

mission to Ruhland, in Germany. A few miles from Wittenburg, a Me 262 from JG 7 shot down two bombers. As the fighter made a third pass at the 'heavies', Capt Edwin Miller of the 83rd FS took a long range shot at it and achieved a few hits that made the fighter dive away. Attempting to stay with his jet-powered quarry, Miller was clocking 500 mph as he chased the German machine through a thin overcast and caught it in a turn. As the pilot straightened up in an attempt to outrun the Mustang, Miller used his deadly K-14 gunsight to strike the jet from 500 yards, slowing it down. He then closed in and hit the fighter solidly, the Me 262 rolling onto its back and diving straight into the ground.

Squadronmate Lt John Kirk spotted another Me 262 as Miller went after his;

'He turned towards us and dove, and I immediately dove after him, full throttle. Red line was 500-505 mph, and I was right on the red line. I decided to chance hitting him, even though you were not supposed to fire your guns at red line speed. I shot off two bursts and the wings didn't come off. I then fired twice more and hit one of the jet's engines, which slowed the fighter up. The pilot started to pull out low, and I gained gun range and put the K-14 on him, and could see hits all around the cockpit. All of a sudden the canopy came off and he came out like he had an ejection seat, flipping past me so close that I thought I would hit him. I filmed the jet going in and exploding.'

A short while later mission leader Conner found Alt Lönnewitz airfield packed with aeroplanes, including several Me 262s. Whilst strafing three jets waiting to take off, Conner's Mustang was hit by flak. Heading east, he crash-landed east of the Oder River in no-man's land. Eventually, Conner was found by Soviet troops and transported to Lvov, then in Poland, then Poltava, in the Ukraine, before finally reaching Moscow, from whence he returned to Duxford on 10 May.

At 1215 hrs Capt Winfield Brown, flying as 82nd FS lead, spotted three Me 262s taking off from Giebelstadt airfield. Diving from 14,000 ft, Brown hit one of the jets but was then forced to break off due to flak. Lt Allen Rosenblum closed on the damaged fighter and shot it down. Lt Robert Anderson chased down a second Me 262, despite his P-51 being hit by flak. Engaging the jet at an altitude of just 50 ft, he watched it explode upon hitting the ground. Lt Walter Bourque, who was 'Blue Three' in the 82nd FS formation, climbed towards what he thought were three P-51s with wing tanks that turned out to be Me 262s. Overtaking several Mustangs from the 339th FG that were also chasing the jets, Bourque got to within firing distance of the last Me 262 and hit it solidly – the fighter spun away out of control.

The following day two more Messerschmitt jet fighters fell to the group in the same area, Lts Eugene Peel and Milton Stutzman of the 82nd FS sharing one and Capt Harold Barnaby of the 83rd FS getting the other Me262 to 'make ace'. He recalled;

'My attention was attracted to Giebelstadt airdrome because of its long runway and the number of jet fighters dispersed around its perimeter. Four Me 262s were parked on the runway ready to take off. After relating this information to "Phoenix Leader", I saw one of the jets taking off from east to west. From 10,000 ft over the western end of the runway, I closed rapidly in a slight left turn as the Me 262 cleared the runway. I was indicating 425 mph and was about 400 yards behind him when I reached his 1000 ft altitude. He was already going at 400 mph despite having been airborne for less than three miles.

'My first burst caused an explosion when it hit his left engine, blowing off parts. Hits in the wings and fuselage convinced the pilot to pull up to 2000 ft and bail out. The Me 262 half-rolled to the right and struck the ground vertically.'

Lt Col Landers led the group again on 30 March, when it helped escort 1320 bombers on a mission to Hamburg. Freed to hunt, Landers turned his pilots toward Kiel. Approaching Rendsburg airfield, in northern Germany, the group CO spotted an Me 262 1000 ft off the ground. Diving from 7000 ft with his wingman Lt Thomas Thain, Landers was able to catch the jet as the pilot made 'suicidal' shallow turns. Both Landers and Thain took turns in shooting at the Me 262, which crashed and burned short of the runway at Hohn.

The following day Lt Wayne Coleman, flying as 82nd FS 'Red Leader' at 15,000 ft near Stendal, spotted two Me 262s on a parallel course to his formation darting in and out of clouds. He then saw two other flights go after a third Me 262, which disappeared into a smoke cloud. Moments later this machine emerged again, so Coleman split-essed into a full power dive. Coming into range of the jet, he set the K-14 gunsight in his cockpit and scored strikes to the canopy and right engine. Breaking left, the jet rolled right and went straight in, exploding on impact. This was Coleman's fourth, and last, victory.

During March the Mustang had revived the fortunes of the 78th, which had flown 25 missions and scored a group record 54 aerial victories and four ground victories, plus nine locomotives destroyed. However, this success had come at a high price, with nine pilots killed in action and one in a flying accident, four captured, three evaders and three wounded in action.

After a week of bad weather, 7 April saw an escort mission to Berlin. North of Dummer Lake, the 83rd FS's 'Blue Leader' and future ace, Lt Francis Harrington, spotted three contrails at 23,000 ft that turned out to be made by Bf 109s, shooting down one. He then engaged some Fw 190s, following one down through a layer of cloud before hitting him hard. The German fighter rolled over and went straight in.

'Yellow Leader', and ace, Capt Robert Green chased after two Bf 109s heading for the bombers. The first one was hit by return fire from several B-17s before it collided with one of them. Dodging the wreckage of the two aircraft, Green went after the second Messerschmitt, shooting out its

The official caption for this candid photograph of 6.5-kill ace Capt Robert Green (left), flight surgeon Capt Kent Hunt (centre) and Capt Edwin Miller (right) of the 83rd FS read as follows. 'Capt Robert I Green of Long Beach, California, desperately hangs on to his "good luck" scarf while Capt Kent N Hunt, a flight surgeon from San Antonio, Texas, tries to remove the neckpiece and Capt Edwin H Miller of Carson City, Nevada, even offers his own as a replacement. Capt Green admits he hasn't washed the scarf for a "couple of years", but he wouldn't fly a mission without it'. The scarf clearly worked as a lucky charm, for Green completed 86 missions totalling 372 hours between July 1944 and April 1945 (*USAAF*)

Aces 1Lt Duncan McDuffie and Capt Dick Hewitt were photographed chatting outside one of the hangars at Duxford in the spring of 1945. The caption accompanying this shot stated, '1Lt Duncan M McDuffie, of Aiken, South Carolina, of the 78th FG, who recently shot down four German fighters in one aerial battle, attaches his good luck charm (a rabbit's foot) to his helmet. Capt Richard A Hewitt, a 78th FG squadron commander from Lewiston, New York, wears a rabbit's foot on his dog tag chain' (*USAAF*)

elevators. The fighter then spun slowly into the ground, taking the pilot with it. Lt Richard Kuehl also attacked a Bf 109 whose pilot quickly bailed out. The 78th FG's 326th, and last, credited aerial victory went to 84th FS pilots Lts Richard Corbett and Henry Slack (who subsequently 'made ace') a short while later when they shared in the destruction of a Bf 109 northeast of Dummer Lake.

8 April was the 78th's second anniversary in combat, and it was observed with an uneventful escort mission to Plauen, in Germany. The mission flown two days later, when bombers targeted Brandenburg-Briest airfield as part of the USAAF's anti-jet campaign, proved to be anything but routine. Departing the bombers after they had dropped their ordnance, the Mustang pilots went hunting. Landers spotted P-47s strafing an aerodrome, and noticed that it was still full of intact aircraft when they departed.

Calling the 83rd and 84th FSs to join him and the 82nd FS, the group worked over Werder airfield, leaving 60 aircraft burning after several passes. No fewer than six of these were claimed by Lt Col Landers, with the 82nd FS being credited with 33 kills, the 83rd FS 11 victories and the 84th FS eight victories. Huie Lamb was one of four pilots from the group to claim four. In fact, only three pilots from the 78th failed to score on 10 April. Lt Herbert Stinson was killed by flak over the airfield, while Lts Roger Spaulding and Richard Kuehl became PoWs – the latter for just 36 hours, as he was rescued by the US Army's 84th Infantry Division and returned to Duxford on 14 April.

On 16 April the 78th flew one of the most important missions in its history, the operation later being described as a 'long, wearisome and hazardous flight deep into enemy territory'. After providing area support to 760 B-17s and B-24s of the 1st and 2nd ADs targeting bridges and marshalling yards in the Regensburg-Straubing-Platting-Landshut area, Landers led the 82nd FS in the hunt for aircraft. Although he soon found Straubing airfield literally jammed with parked aircraft, they would not burn when attacked due to the Luftwaffe's by now chronic lack of fuel. Other airfields were strafed near Marienbad. Three Mustangs were downed and two pilots killed in abortive strafing attempts at Straubing, Ganacker and Marienbad.

Landers then turned the group towards Prague, in Czechoslovakia, where intelligence had reported that hundreds of German aircraft had recently arrived seeking shelter from the advancing Allied armies. Arriving over Praha-Kakewice airfield, north of Prague, at 1530 hrs, Landers observed 80 aircraft scattered all over the base. On his first pass he lit up four He 177s, and on his second he burned two more – Landers was ultimately credited with the destruction of nine Heinkel bombers. The first two flights across the airfield set 13 aircraft on fire, and after four passes by the 83rd and 84th FSs, 50 aircraft were identified as being ablaze. As they flew off, only three German aircraft remained intact. 'Blue Flight' of the 82nd FS quickly finished those off to give the group a 100 per cent score.

Aside from Landers, other high-scorers at Praha-Kakewice included the 84th's Lt Clyde Taylor with nine kills, Lts Danford Josey and Neal Hepner with five each and Lt Henry Slack with four. Staff pilot Maj Gillespie Bryan also claimed four kills.

Other pilots who could not attack Praha-Kakewice through the smoke hit nearby Prague-Letnany airfield instead. After three passes the minimal flak at the base had been silenced, allowing the attacking pilots to fly a left-hand gunnery pattern for a full 25 minutes. Many of the 70 aircraft on the airfield would not burn for lack of fuel, however. Nevertheless, the 83rd's Capt Edward Kulik claimed

seven victories and Lts Anthony Colletti, Donald DeVilliers, Gene Doss, Duncan McDuffie and Dale Sweat were credited with five apiece.

With their ammunition all but exhausted, and with only enough fuel for the return flight, the pilots from the 78th left 135 German aircraft smashed and burning in their wake in Czechoslovakia – the record high strafing score for the Eighth Air Force in World War 2, which earned the group a second USAAF Distinguished Unit Citation. This mission also proved to be one of the longest flown by any American fighter group in the ETO, having lasted seven hours and forty minutes.

An escort to Dresden the next day provided the 78th with its final strafing successes of the conflict when 'Red Flight' of the 84th FS chased 'bandits' that were friendly, then spotted an airfield with 30 aircraft parked on it. Encountering very little flak, Lts Danford Josey, William McClellan and John Sole made six passes that left nine aircraft on fire and ten damaged, including a captured B-17 in German markings. Staff pilot Maj Gillespie Bryan also claimed two victories and three damaged.

The 82nd and 83rd FSs, meanwhile, had returned to Prague, where Capt Richard Hewitt spotted and chased two Me 262s that headed for Kralupy airfield. He shot down the second one moments before it landed and then targeted the lead jet before it could turn off the runway. The fighter flown by Hewitt's wingman, Lt Allen Rosenblum, was badly hit over the field during the attack, however. Yet despite having his engine knocked out, as he pulled up he saw a trainer on the ground and strafed it just seconds before he crashed! Hewitt watched as Rosenblum's P-51 skidded across the aerodrome at more than 300 mph, careened through two hedgerows and disappeared into a stand of trees. Amazingly, Rosenblum survived to become a PoW. He was one of two 82nd FS pilots captured that day after falling victim to flak.

Unfortunately, Hewitt did not receive credit for the destruction of the airborne Me 262, which would have been his fifth aerial victory, as Rosenblum was unavailable to support his claim.

20 April saw Eighth Air Force HQ order a ban on further strafing attacks, which frustrated the 78th FG the following day when it spotted 20 Me 262s on the autobahn southeast of Munich. After the bombers turned away, the three squadrons started for home. The weather became progressively

1Lt Anthony Palopoli joined the 83rd FS in October 1944 and was eventually assigned P-51D-25 44-72146 *"Little Joe"*, which he named for his younger brother Joe. Seen here with a canine friend, Palopoli used 44-72146 to destroy three Ju 87s during the Prague strafing mission of 16 April 1945, and narrowly escaped crashing in Germany during a snowstorm the following day (*USAAF*)

Capt Dorian Ledington of the 84th FS also scored three strafing victories on the Prague mission of 16 April 1945, which combined with his two aerial successes in June 1944 to give him ace status. On 21 April Ledington was leading his squadron when it ran into bad weather over Germany. Trying to drop down below the rain and thunderstorms west of Koblenz, he hit a tree and crashed to his death (*USAAF via John M Dibbs/Plane Picture Company*)

On 1 June Duxford was opened to the British public to mark Air Force Day, and some 5000 visitors toured the airfield viewing both aircraft and equipment. Amongst the fighters on display was P-51D-10 44-14251 *Contrary Mary*, assigned to Lt Col Roy Caviness. Formerly CO of the 361st FG, Caviness relieved Lt Col Landers of command of the 78th FG on 28 June 1945. Note the 110-gallon metal tanks underwing. Caviness had brought this aircraft with him from the 361st FG, where it was assigned to the 376th FS (*USAAF*)

On 7 June 1945 officers and enlisted men of the 78th FG paraded under sunny Cambridgeshire skies for the very last time, their P-51D/Ks being neatly lined up at Duxford for a final inspection. The newest of these aircraft would be mothballed for shipment to depots, while the rest would be scrapped (*USAAF*)

worse, however, and by the time pilots from the 84th had fought their way through rain and thunderstorms, they were at just 2000 ft west of Koblenz. At that point they hit a solid front, with zero ceiling and visibility. Leading the squadron, ace Capt Dorian Ledington tried to drop down below the front but hit a tree and crashed to his death. Out of fuel, Lt John Sole bailed out at 300 ft and fell to his death when his parachute failed to deploy. Finally, staff pilot Lt Col Leonard Marshall, who was leading the group that day, flew into overcast conditions at 28,000 ft upside down. His body and non-deployed parachute were discovered by US infantrymen one week later.

25 April saw the 78th FG fly its final mission, escorting 11 Lancasters of No 617 Sqn sent to destroy Hitler's mountain residence, the *Berghof*, in Berchtesgaden with 12,000-lb 'Tallboy' bombs. Capt Huie Lamb flew a special unarmed two-seat P-51D with group flight surgeon Ben Pentecost in the back. After seeing the Lancasters safely away from the target, the group provided escort for B-24s hitting marshalling yards at Salzberg. Escort complete, the 78th crossed the Belgian coast at 1350 hrs and 77 of the 78 aircraft sent aloft were on the ground at Duxford by 1440 hrs. Sadly, Lt Edward Carroll of the 82nd FS perished when his fighter crashed in fog near Sawston, in Cambridgeshire.

The monthly victory tally for April was five aerial kills and 202 strafing victories scored during 18 missions, for seven pilots killed and six captured.

On 8 May 1945, VE Day was quietly celebrated with free beer at the Officers' and NCOs' Clubs and the enlisted club, Duffy's Tavern. An open-air dance turned into a songfest due to a lack of women. Lt Col John Landers departed on 28 May, being replaced by Lt Col Roy Caviness, former commander of the 361st FG. Air Force Day on 1 June was celebrated with an open house that drew more than 5000 visitors to Duxford from the local area. On 10 July the 78th suffered its final fatality when Capt James Farmer of the 84th FS perished in a flying accident.

Before the group could prepare itself for transfer to the Pacific, the war with Japan ended on 15 August.

On 1 September orders reached Duxford that the 78th was to return to the United States for disbandment. All P-51s were flown to Atcham depot, after which group personnel boarded the ocean liner *Queen Mary* on 11 October and arrived in New York Harbor five days later. The 78th FG was disbanded at Camp Kilmer on 18 October 1945 – the site from which it had departed for England 35 months previously. Duxford was returned to RAF control on 1 December 1945.

APPENDICES

Aces of the 78th FG

Ranking	Name	Unit(s)	Aerial Victories	Strafing Victories	Final Score
1	Col John D Landers	49th FG/357th FG/78th FG	14.5	20	34.5*
2	Capt Alwin M Juchheim	83rd FS	9	6	15
3	Maj Quince L Brown	84th FS	12.333	2	14.333
4	1Lt Francis E Harrington	83rd FS	4	8	12
5	Lt Col Olin E Gilbert	78th FG	2	9.5	11.5
6	1Lt John A Kirk	83rd FS	4	8	12
7	Capt Charles M Peal	83rd FS	2	8	10
8	Capt Duncan M McDuffie	83rd FS	4	5	9
10	Lt Col Eugene P Roberts	84th FS/78th FG	9	-	9
11	1Lt Clyde L Taylor	84th FS	-	9	9
12	Lt Col Joseph Myers	55th FG/78th FG	4.5	4	8.5**
13	1Lt Henry R Slack	84th FS	1.5	7	8.5
14	Maj Richard A Hewitt	82nd FS	4	4.333	8.333
15	Capt John J Hockery	82nd FS	7	1.1	8.1
16	Lt Col Richard E Conner	84th FS/78th FG	4.5	3.5	8
17	1Lt Danford E Josey	84th FS	-	8	8
18	Lt Col William H Julian	83rd FS	5	3	8
19	1Lt Richard L Messinger	83rd FS	-	8	8
20	Capt James W Wilkinson	82nd FS	6	2	8
21	Lt Col Jack L Oberhansly	82nd FS/78th FG	6	1.6	7.6
22	Maj Norman D Munson	82nd FS	-	7.5	7.5
23	1Lt Neal Hepner	84th FS	-	7	7
24	Capt Edward R Kulik	83rd FS	-	7	7
25	Capt Peter E Pompetti	84th FS	5	2	7
26	Maj Raymond E Smith	84th FS	1	6	7
27	Capt Robert T Green	83rd FS	4.5	2	6.5
28	Lt Col Benjamin I. Mayo	82nd FS/84th FS	4	2.5	6.5
29	Capt Benjamin M Watkins	82nd FS	2	4.5	6.5
30	1Lt Robert R Bosworth	82nd FS	1	5	6
31	1Lt Gerald E Brasher	82nd FS	1	5	6
32	Maj Gillespie Bryan	78th FG/84th FS	-	6	6
33	1Lt Anthony T Colletti	83rd FS	1	5	6
34	1Lt Louis DeAnda	84th FS	-	6	6
35	Capt Donald J DeVilliers	83rd FS	-	6	6
36	Capt Herbert K Shope	82nd FS	-	6	6
37	1Lt Grant M Turley	82nd FS	6	-	6
38	1Lt Warren M Wesson	82nd FS	4	2	6
39	1Lt Merle R Capp	82nd FS/84th FS	2	3.5	5.5
40	Capt Huie H Lamb	82nd FS	2.5	3	5.5
41	1Lt Eugene L Peel	82nd FS	0.5	5	5.5
42	Capt Harold T Barnaby	83rd FS	4	1	5
43	Capt Robert R Bonebrake	83rd FS	3	2	5
44	Capt Charles W DeWitt	82nd FS	-	5	5
45	1Lt Gene C Doss	83rd FS	-	5	5
46	Capt Dorian Ledington	84th FS	2	3	5
47	Capt Charles P London	83rd FS	5	-	5
48	2Lt Charles E Parmelee	84th FS	3	2	5
49	1Lt Richard E Phaneuf	83rd FS	-	5	5
50	Maj Jack C Price	84th FS	5	-	5
51	1Lt Dale S Sweat	83rd FS	-	5	5

Notes

* Landers scored six aerial victories with 49th FG (SWPA), five aerial and four strafing victories with 55th FG (ETO) and one aerial and one strafing victories with 357th FG (ETO)

** Myers scored three aerial victories with 55th FG (ETO)

1

P-47C-5 41-6335 *EL JEEPO* of Capt Charles London, 83rd FS, Duxford, July 1943

One of the original members of the 78th who remained as 'Red Flight' leader in the 83rd FS following the transferring of all of the group's P-38s and most of its pilots to North Africa in January 1943, London scored three kills on separate missions in late June and early July 1943. I Iis double on 30 July 1943 made him VIII Fighter Command's first ace. His P-47C-5 is depicted here as it appeared in late July after he had 'made ace', newly painted with red-surround insignia in five locations. London claimed all of his aerial successes in 41-6335.

2

P-47C-5 41-6630 *Spokane Chief* of Maj Eugene Roberts, 84th FS, Duxford, July 1943

Another of the 78th FG's original pilots, Gene Roberts was CO of the 84th FS from August 1942 through to 28 September 1943, when he became a staff officer with the group. Seen here fitted with a cumbersome, unpressurised, belly tank, 41-6630 was credited with seven victories while assigned to Roberts.

3

P-47C-5 41-6393 *"Axe the Axis"* of 2Lt Peter Pompetti, 84th FS, Duxford, September 1943

Originally a junior wingman who joined the 78th following the removal of its P-38s and pilots, Peter Pompetti was one of the most aggressive aviators in the group. He scored his first victory, in this aircraft, on 30 July 1943 whilst flying as Quince Brown's wingman. Pompetti was not one to wait for his seniors to decide whether to go after enemy fighters once he had spotted them, and he was nearly thrown out of the group in the autumn of 1943 for his aggressiveness. Pompetti claimed four destroyed and two damaged in this aircraft, which he flew in combat for more than ten months.

4

P-47D-1 42-7883 *IRON ASS* of Maj Jack Oberhansly, 83rd FS, Duxford, November 1943

One of the first pilots assigned to the 78th PG at Hamilton Field, California, Oberhansly subsequently commanded the 83rd FS from 17 August 1943 through to 18 May 1944. 42-7883 is shown here as it appeared in late 1943, with blue and white 'star-and-bar' insignia in five positions with over-painted red surrounds. Oberhansly claimed two victories and one probable in this aircraft.

5

P-47D-6 42-74641 *Feather Merchant II* of Maj Jack Price, 84th FS, Duxford, November 1943

Another 78th FG original, Jack Price scored his first two victories in the epic mission of 30 July 1943. He replaced Gene Roberts as CO of the 84th FS on 28 September 1943 when the latter was transferred to VII Fighter Command HQ. Remaining in command until 25 February 1944, Price claimed five victories exactly. His last two successes, on 26 November 1943 near Paris, came at the controls of 42-74641.

6

P-47D-6 42-74753 *OKIE* of 1Lt Quince Brown, 84th FS, Duxford, January 1944

Brown was among the first replacement pilots to join the 78th FG with formal training in how to fly the P-47. Arriving in April 1943 after a year as a flight instructor, he was immediately made an element leader, and later a flight leader, by Gene

Roberts. Note that *OKIE* had earlier 'barless' insignia in five locations, with 'stars and bars' on the wing uppersurfaces and fuselage insignia. On the wing undersides the 'stars and bars' retained their red surrounds. 42-74753 saw considerable action in the frontline, Brown claiming 7.333 aerial victories with it between 27 September 1943 and 30 March 1944.

7

P-47D-2 42-7998 *Kitty* of 2Lt Grant Turley, 82nd FS, Duxford, February 1944

Grant Turley came to the 78th FG in the autumn of 1943. He scored his first two victories on 10 February 1944, two more the following day and then 'made ace' on the 20th of that same month. Claiming his last officially recognised kill on 24 February, Turley got into a turning fight with two Fw 190s on 6 March after the 82nd FS had come to the rescue of the 83rd FS when it was bounced by 25 Focke-Wulf fighters over Steinhuder Lake. Turley, flying 42-7998, downed one of the Fw 190s (although this seventh success was never officially credited to him) just before being shot down by the second German fighter.

8

P-47D-5 42-8530 *Jeanie -V.O.S.-* of 1Lt Warren Wesson, 82nd FS, Duxford, February 1944

Warren Wesson flew as a wingman in the 82nd FS, claiming his first kill – on 26 November 1943 – in this aircraft during an escort mission to Montdidier, near Paris. Engaging an Fw 190 at long range, Wesson watched as the fighter 'turned and flew right through my fire'. He achieved further aerial strafing successes during February 1944, completing his tour in May of that year.

9

P-47C-2 41-6260 of 1Lt Ernest Russell, 84th FS, Duxford, March 1944

'Ernie' Russell joined the 78th in the summer of 1943, only two months after his 19th birthday. Although not an ace, he flew as wingman for Lt Quince Brown. Eventually promoted to element leader, Russell experienced his most memorable mission on 16 March 1944. Completing escort duty, he followed Brown in an attack on Saint-Dizier airfield southeast of Paris. Russell, in 41-6260, destroyed a taxiing Bf 110 while Brown shot a Bf 109 down that was in the landing pattern. He also destroyed a Ju 88 that was taking off, as well as shooting down a second Bf 109 and an Fw 190. Russell returned to the United States just before D-Day, and later trained Tuskegee airmen.

10

P-47D-21 42-25698 *Okie* of Capt Quince Brown, 84th FS, Duxford, May 1944

Brown took delivery of his second *Okie* in May 1944, flying it until the end of his first tour in July – he claimed no victories with the fighter, however. 42-25698 was one of the first natural metal finish Thunderbolts to arrive at Duxford. Returning to the 78th for a second tour on 28 August, Brown was promoted to major and made CO of the 84th FS. He also re-took possession of this aircraft, although it was soon replaced by P-47D-28 44-19569. Brown was shot down by flak in the latter fighter just nine days after rejoining the 78th FG.

11

P-47D-21 42-26020 *Lady Jane* of Capt Alwin Juchheim, 83rd FS, Duxford, May 1944

The 78th FG's second-ranking ace, Juchheim joined the group on 30 November 1943 and went on to fly 76 missions prior to becoming a PoW on 28 May 1944 after his P-47 collided with a P-51 from the Ninth Air Force over Germany. Juchheim claimed three aerial victories, one probable and one damaged in 42-26020 between 30 April and 25 May – he also shared in the destruction of an He 111 on the ground at Saint-Dizier.

12

P-47D-21 serial unknown *PIN UP GIRL* of Capt James Wilkinson, 82nd FS, Duxford, May 1944

Briefly serving with the 4th FG until he was injured in a flying accident in April 1943, Wilkinson joined the 78th five months later. He claimed his first success on 1 December 1943 in the original *PIN UP GIRL*, P-47D-2 42-7954. Wilkinson's remaining victories were scored in a variety of Thunderbolts, including this aircraft, whose serial remains unknown. He was killed in a flying accident in bad weather in Wales just 48 hours prior to D-Day, Wilkinson's fighter (P-47D-22 42-26387) crashing into a mist-shrouded hillside near Llandovery.

13

P-47D-25 42-26671 *No Guts – No Glory!* of Capt Ben Mayo, 82nd FS, Duxford, June 1944

Ben Mayo spent time as CO of both the 82nd and 84th FSs during his six-month tour with the group. He also claimed aerial victories with both squadrons. Mayo flew this aircraft while leading the 82nd FS from 8 June to 14 July, hence its full D-Day stripes. He probably used this fighter to claim a Bf 109 destroyed over Montdidier on 20 June and an Fw 190 damaged over Saint-Quentin on 1 July. The 42-26671 was subsequently camouflaged in late July.

14

P-47D-25 42-27339 of Maj Joseph Myers, 82nd FS, Duxford, September 1944

A veteran of a 130-mission tour with the P-38-equipped 55th FG, with whom he had claimed three aerial victories, Maj Myers joined the 78th FG as the new CO of the 82nd FS in August 1944. Issued with 42-27339, he used the aircraft to share in the destruction (on 28 August 1944) of the first Me 262 to fall to a fighter pilot of the Eighth Air Force. Myers also destroyed three He 111s with this machine during a strafing attack on Meinbullen airfield on 10 September and shot down a Bf 109 over Leipzig on 7 October.

15

P-47D-28 42-28878 *Eileen* of 1Lt Frank Oiler, 84th FS, Duxford, September 1944

Frank Oiler joined the 78th shortly after D-Day and flew as a wingman and, later, element leader in the 84th FS. He named his first P-47D-21 for his girlfriend, as was his follow-on D-28, depicted here. Oiler failed to claim any aerial or strafing successes in the Thunderbolt, but shot down an Fw 190 and destroyed an Me 410 and a Ju 88 on the ground whilst flying the Mustang in early 1945.

16

P-47D-25RE 44-19930 of 1Lt Wayne Coleman, 82nd FS, Duxford, September 1944

1Lt Wayne Coleman claimed three Fw 190s shot down over Hersfeld, Germany, on 9 September 1944 whilst flying this machine. He would have to wait until 31 March 1945 to claim his next success, shooting down a Me 262 over Stendal. Coleman never got the chance to claim that all-important fifth victory prior to VE Day.

17

P-47D-26 42-28422 of 2Lt Huie Lamb, 82nd FS, Duxford, October 1944

Huie Lamb claimed the first two of his 5.5 victories in this aircraft, downing a Bf 109 over Hamburg on 12 October 1944 and a Me 262 over its airfield at Bohmte three days later. 42-28422 was hit hard by flak as he raced over the base, but Lamb stayed low and managed to fly out of the flak corridor and back to Duxford.

18

P-51D-20 44-63286 *Etta Jeanne* of 1Lt Huie Lamb, 82nd FS, Duxford, December 1944

On Lamb's first mission (an escort to Nuremburg) in the P-51D on 29 December 1944, the engine in this aircraft overheated during the return leg due to his unfamiliarity with the Mustang, and he was forced to ditch in the English Channel. His wingman had no radio, and made his way to Martlesham Heath, from whence he led a Walrus back to the crash location. Lamb managed to survive 45 minutes in the freezing water, although he was first thought to have succumbed to exposure by his rescuers when they hauled him into the Walrus. Flying P-51K-5 44-11631 *Etta Jeanne II*, Lamb would share in the destruction of an Ar 234 jet bomber on 19 March and claim three strafing victories on 10 April.

19

P-51D-20 44-63209 *Sherman was Right!* of 1Lt Frank Oiler, 84th FS, Duxford, January 1945

Frank Oiler was one of many Duxford-based pilots unhappy to trade the P-47 for the P-51D, but he quickly became a believer in the new fighter when, during his first mission in this Mustang on 6 January 1945, he out-turned two Bf 109s that 'had me dead to rights'. He shot down an Fw 190 eight days later. 44-63209 was subsequently written off on 4 March when Lt Louis Hereford became lost in bad weather southeast of Nordlingen, Germany, and was killed when the fighter crashed.

20

P-51D-20 44-63712 *FLY'N TIME BOMB* of Maj Ray Smith, 84th FS, Duxford, February 1945

The nickname applied to this P-51D is a 'tip of the hat' from the personnel of the 84th FS to the many mechanical problems and accidents experienced by the group during its troubled transition to the Mustang during the bitter winter of 1944/45. In this case, the name memorialises Ray Smith's crash on takeoff on 6 January 1945 – the first day the 84th FS had enough serviceable P-51s available to participate in a mission. Smith's fighter experienced an engine failure shortly after takeoff, and he received facial cuts in the resulting crash landing. *FLY'N TIME BOMB* was the nickname given to his replacement aircraft. Smith served with the 84th from October 1943 to April 1945, and claimed his solitary aerial victory and five strafing kills flying the P-47 in 1944. Note also the impressive tally of locomotives destroyed that adorns 44-63712.

21

P-51D-20 44-63187 *Bum Steer* of 1Lt Earl Stier, 84th FS, Duxford, February 1945

During the 78th's first mission to Berlin on 3 February 1945, 1Lt Earl Stier's *Bum Steer* was hit by flak while strafing the airfield at Lüneburg. Several 20 mm shells damaged his radiator and blew off the upper half of his fin and rudder. Stier also damaged his left horizontal stabiliser and elevator when he clipped a tree with his left wingtip battling to control his damaged machine. Stier managed to remain airborne and fly 450 miles back to Duxford, fighting the aeroplane all the way as it corkscrewed through the sky and continually tried to fall off on its left wing. Arriving over the airfield, Stier managed to get the gear down and make a rough landing to the cheers of 300 groundcrewmen. 44-63187 subsequently became the last fighter to be lost by the 78th FG at Duxford when Capt James Farmer crashed in it and was killed on 10 July 1945.

22

P-51D-20 44-72233 of Lt Col Richard Conner, 82nd FS, Duxford, March 1945

Richard Conner became a locomotive 'ace' during the fierce battles following D-Day, and took command of the 82nd FS on 28 August 1944. On 7 October during an escort to Leipzig, he shot down the fourth Me 262 credited to an Eighth Air Force pilot. Conner began a second tour on 17 February 1945. On 21 March, leading the group on an escort mission to Dresden, Conner spotted an airfield nearby on which were parked a number of Me 262s. He managed to set three of them on fire during his first strafing pass, with the third jet exploding just as he flew over it, knocking out the engine of 44-72233. Conner managed to stay with the fighter long enough to get to no man's land between German and Soviet lines, where he crashed east of the Oder River. He was rescued by Soviet troops and eventually transported to Moscow. Conner returned to Duxford on 10 May, three days after the war had ended.

23

P-51D-15 44-15745 of 1Lt Walter Bourque, 82nd FS, Duxford, April 1945

Flying element lead to squadron CO Capt Dick Hewitt, Bourque scored his first victory on 19 March 1945 when the 78th discovered 125 Bf 109s gathering for an attack on the bomber formation the group was escorting. Two days later he shot down a Me 262 from a formation of four that he attacked, Bourque's victim being one of five Messerschmitt jets credited to the 78th as shot down that day. All of Bourque's successes were claimed in this unnamed aircraft.

24

P-51D-20 44-64147 *BIG DICK* of Capt Dick Hewitt, 82nd FS, Duxford, April 1945

Dick Hewitt first joined the 78th FG as a replacement pilot in August 1943, and after completing his first tour just before D-Day, he returned in July 1944 for a second tour. On 21 March 1945 Hewitt became commander of the 82nd FS. Two days earlier he had shot down a pair of Bf 109s in this aircraft, and he went on to destroy a Me 262 on the ground with it on 17 April. Minutes earlier he had shot down another jet just before it landed, but this claim went unconfirmed due to his wingman being shot down and captured – the latter was the only witness to this kill.

25

P-51D-20 44-72099 "*LITTLE CHIC*" of 1Lt Warren Blodgett, 84th FS, Duxford, April 1945

Blodgett, who flew 45 missions between November 1944 and April 1945, claimed four strafing kills in this aircraft in the final months of the war in the ETO. He was one of the few wingmen to achieve multiple successes in the Mustang.

26

P-51D-20 44-63620 *SMALL BOY HERE* of 1Lt John Kirk, 83rd FS, Duxford, April 1945

Kirk considered himself lucky to survive his tour, as two of his roommates were lost ditching in the English Channel. The group's sixth ranking ace, Kirk was nearly shot down strafing an aerodrome at Potsdam during the 78th FG's first mission to Berlin on 3 February 1945. Exactly three weeks later, while strafing a train, he was hit by flak that blew open the gun cover on his right wing. Kirk flew home despite ammunition flapping in the slipstream against the wing the whole way. One of the highlights of his 49-mission tour was the downing of a Me 262 in this very aircraft on 21 March after a wild maximum-speed chase. Despite his numerous close shaves in the fighter, Kirk said 'the P-51 was an aeroplane that made the pilot feel confident'.

27

P-51D-20 44-63191 *Lucky Baby* of 1Lt William McClellan, 84th FS, Duxford, April 1945

On 17 April 1945, while leading 'Red Flight' of the 84th FS in this aircraft, 1Lt William McClellan spotted a lightly-defended German airfield west of Dresden and led his flight on six passes. The 13 aircraft destroyed and 13 damaged (McClellan was credited with three destroyed and four damaged) were the last successes credited to the 78th FG in World War 2.

28

P-51K-5 44-11573 *THE GREEN HORNET* of Capt Robert Green, 83rd FS, Duxford, April 1945

An 86-mission veteran who served with the 83rd FS from July 1944 to April 1945, Green finished his lengthy tour with 4.5 aerial and two strafing victories to his name. He claimed his last victory on 7 April 1945 in the aircraft over Dummer Lake, the Bf 109 he downed being amongst the final five aerial successes credited to the 78th FG.

29

P-51D-20 44-72218 *Big Beautiful Doll* of Lt Col John Landers, 78th FG, Duxford, April 1945

Lt Col John Landers relieved Col Fred Gray as group CO on 17 February 1945, and subsequently led the group through to war's end. One of the most experienced fighter pilots in the USAAF, he enjoyed considerable success at the controls of this machine as he led the 78th on several memorable missions in the spring of 1945. Always in the vanguard of the action, Landers claimed 3.5 aerial kills and 15 strafing victories between 2 March and 16 April.

30

P-51D-15 44-72146 "*Little Joe*" of 1Lt Anthony Palopoli. 83rd FS, Duxford, April 1945

Palopoli, who joined the 78th in October 1944, named his Mustang for his younger brother Joe, also applying the insignia of the unit (70th Infantry Division 'Trail Blazers') in which his brother served on the nose of this machine. Palopoli used 44-72146 to destroy three aircraft during the Prague strafing mission of 16 April 1945, and narrowly escaped crashing in Germany during a snowstorm the following day.

INDEX